Eucharist and Sacrifice

GUSTAF AULÉN

Emanuel Hildebrand, Bp.

EUCHARIST

and

SACRIFICE

Translated by
ERIC H. WAHLSTROM

MUHLENBERG PRESS • PHILADELPHIA

Translated from *För eder utgiven*
by Gustaf Aulén
Diakonistyrelses Bokförlag, Stockholm, 1956

Preface

The purpose of this little book is to shed some light on the modern, ecumenical discussions of the Lord's Supper. We desire above all to deal with those problems about which men hold different opinions. We have not deemed it necessary to provide complete references to all the literature on the subject. What is important is not to note and discuss all the documents, but to define the fundamental ideas presented by various people, and to subject these ideas to a critical analysis both historically and in principle. Free and open criticism, even in the form of self-analysis, is a vital condition for all ecumenical endeavors. Without it a study of this nature would be worthless. But it would be worthless, too, if this criticism were not also positive, i.e., ecumenical. The purpose of this book is not to close doors but to open them.

Lund, All Saints' Day, 1955. Gustaf Aulén

Contents

Part II
The Reformation

Part III
The Teaching of the New Testament

Part IV
Conclusions

Introduction

Current Interest in the Lord's Supper

In recent times the Lord's Supper has become the object of intense interest both from a practical and from a theoretical point of view, in theology as well as in the life of the church. Everywhere in the Christian world we encounter efforts to renew and strengthen the observance of the sacrament, not least within those communions where the eucharist traditionally has not been emphasized. Theology, likewise, has become more interested in clarifying the significance of the sacrament. Many factors have been responsible for this renewal of interest. We will discuss only three of these: liturgical renaissance, present-day biblical research, and the ecumenical movement.

1. *Liturgical Renaissance*

The significance of liturgy for the worship life of the church has become more generally recognized. A strong movement of liturgical renewal pervades practically the whole Christian world. This movement is found even within communions which in the past have shown little interest in liturgy. The conception that liturgy and preaching represent conflicting functions has been given up, and it has become generally recognized that these two functions complement and strengthen one another.

Since the eucharist is the center of the church's liturgy, it is evident that this liturgical renewal finds its focus in the sacrament. But it is also clear that the liturgical pattern of the communion service is closely related to and dependent upon the current theological interpretation of the sacrament. Consequently it is not surprising that a growing number of works dealing with the theology of worship have recently appeared.

An attempt to describe the liturgical renaissance within the various communions would require a large book indeed. We have to confine ourselves to a very brief survey. It should be emphasized that this movement is common to all Christian churches. In the case of Reformed communions the movement in many instances represents a new orientation. A significant work has been accomplished and is continuing among the Reformed churches both in Europe and America. In part the result has been the adoption of a new order of service as in the case of the Church of Scotland, which in the Book of Common Order of 1940 has received a new order of service with a much richer liturgy than in previous times.

We are well aware of the importance which the liturgical problems have assumed within the Anglican communion. The Church of England has for a long time been engaged in intensive work on liturgical renewal, which has been both stimulated and hindered by opposing tendencies within the church itself. This work has not produced any official result, since Parliament, which makes the final decision, rejected the proposed Order of Service of 1927 and 1928, after it had been accepted by the ecclesiastical authorities. But the labor has not been entirely in vain. In spite of parliamentary rejection the church has found ways and means to utilize the results of this work in the worship of the church. Furthermore, the rejection was received favorably by many, since the proposed order was the result of so much compromise that no one was completely satisfied. The Church of England also has produced a number of theological works with a liturgical orientation. We will have to consider many of these in the course of our study.

Among the churches which, contrary to the Reformer's desire, are called Lutheran, we find a vigorous development in liturgical renewal on the Continent, in America, and in Scandinavia. Here we have to confine ourselves to a few remarks on the development in the Church of Sweden. The Book of Service which was given to the church in 1811 under the influence of the Enlightenment was the most meager in her history. The new handbook of 1894 was an indication that the liturgical low had been passed, and that the church desired to enrich its order of service. Since then the work on the liturgy has continued. The last official result, the Handbook of 1942, presents a much richer content, not least in respect to the liturgical service of Holy Communion. The difference is not merely quantitative but also qualitative, especially noticeable in the stronger emphasis on the eucharistic element.

We may also note a lively activity directed toward a liturgical renewal within the Roman Catholic church. It is, of course, not a question of changing the liturgical formulas; in that respect Rome represents a static permanence. But efforts are made to enhance the communion service and to find ways in which the laity may actively participate. Liturgical interest appears also in the attempts to clarify the real significance of the mass on the basis of the teaching of Thomas Aquinas and the foremost fathers, and to eliminate conceptions regarded as unworthy and misleading. Pius XII in his encyclical, *Mediator Dei,* 1947, has sought to regulate these attempts and to set up boundaries which must not be transgressed.

2. *Modern Biblical Research*

Biblical scholarship has to a large degree served to focus attention on the Lord's Supper. Modern exegetical research takes quite a different view of the place of the cultus within the ancient church from that customary in exegetical works during the nineteenth century. A radical change has taken place. Earlier exegesis regarded the cult and everything connected with it as secondary and nonessential; but modern exegesis, on the contrary, strongly accentuates the central position of the cult. It maintains that the worship life of the early church had its center in the celebration of the Lord's Supper. There are many differences in regard to the details, but complete agreement on this central point: the ancient church appears as a worshiping fellowship (*koinonia*), and the Lord's Supper is both the means of creating this fellowship and an expression of its present reality. This new insight has come because modern exegesis, in contrast to earlier individualistic interpretations, has discovered the inseparable connection between Christ and his church. The work of Christ created the church, and the church lives in an indissoluble union with Christ. The church is "the body of Christ." To become a Christian is to be made a member of this body of Christ. The fellowship of the new age is characterized by the fact that it receives its life and righteousness from Christ. Worship and eucharist stand in the context of this perspective.

It is obvious that by opening up such a perspective modern biblical research has greatly contributed to focusing attention on the eucharist. It poses especially searching questions for those communions in which Holy Communion has occupied a more or less obscure place. It is also clear that what happens in this area of biblical research becomes of great importance for ecumenical problems. This is especially true because this new exegetical attitude is not confined to any one communion and its theology, but affects them all, even though the traditional emphases of the various churches also play a part.

3. Ecumenical Conversations

The ecumenical movement is one of the most remarkable events within the life of the church in modern times. It began in the second decade of this century and has grown in momentum ever since. We will not attempt to enumerate the results achieved. Even if these results appear rather meager to many enthusiastic participants and spectators, it cannot be denied that we have entered upon a new direction. The advance is no longer toward an increasing fragmentation, as it has been for several centuries, but rather toward an increasing unity. The day of isolated denominations is past. New contacts have been established which have been unknown since the time when the divisions appeared.

The ecumenical movement accentuates the Lord's Supper in two respects. At every ecumenical gathering the Lord's Supper appears as a witness and as an accuser: a witness to the unity which ought to find visible expression, and an accuser against the schisms which exist. There are, of course, many aspects of Holy Communion. But no matter how many different opinions there may be concerning its significance, all agree that Holy Communion is the sacrament of Christian fellowship and Christian unity. Consequently, when Christians meet to discuss the divisions of Christianity, attention is immediately focused on the sacrament. The eucharist appears as an accuser because the participants cannot celebrate the sacrament together. The reasons for avoiding the celebration may be of different kinds. The arguments may be derived from "Faith" or from "Order"; or it might be argued that the presupposition for a celebration of the eucharist is a united church, and that there is, therefore, an inner contradiction in a common celebration of the sacrament while the churches remain divided. Whatever reasons may be given, the fact remains that this attitude toward the sacrament of unity becomes a demonstration of the divisions of Christianity. An ecumenical fellowship cannot escape the painful consciousness of this situation. The Report of the Conference on Faith and Order at Lund in 1952, states: [1] "When we are unable to share together in the Lord's Supper the pain and scandal of our divisions is most severely felt because we seek the one Lord, and know that we should be able to partake as brethren in the family of God at one Table."

If every ecumenical meeting automatically raises the question of "intercommunion," the problem cannot be isolated and regarded

[1] Oliver S. Tomkins (ed.), *Third World Conference on Faith and Order Held at Lund 1952* (London: Student Christian Movement, 1953), p. 53. Cited hereafter as *Lund 1952*.

merely as a technical and organizational question. The differences in regard to the practice of communion which make themselves so painfully evident bring to a focus the whole problem of the significance of the sacrament. It is clear, especially in an ecumenical situation, that Holy Communion, or rather the various interpretations of it, was the chief cause of the deepest divisions in the church at the time of the Reformation. The meaning and significance of Holy Communion become inevitably a principal subject of discussion in ecumenical meetings. The conversations which have been held on this subject have to a very large degree been concerned with the idea of sacrifice in the eucharist. Serious attempts have been made to avoid the old, stereotyped approaches to the subject. Fruitful discussions across "the boundaries" have actually taken place. It is imperative that these discussions become the object of a positive and critical analysis.

Part I

Ecumenical Discussions About the Lord's Supper

1

Conference Pronouncements

(STATEMENTS BY ECUMENICAL CONFERENCES)

The modern ecumenical conversations about Holy Communion have been concerned with two principal ideas: the problem of intercommunion, and the interpretation of the significance of the sacrament. In the latter case the question of the element of sacrifice has been prominent. A whole literature has appeared concerning the difficulties and possibilities of intercommunion. This book, however, is not intended to deal specifically with that subject. We are interested exclusively in the central theological problems of the interpretation of the Lord's Supper. Since there is, nevertheless, a certain connection between these two sets of problems, we shall consider briefly the discussions held and the pronouncements made by the conferences. It may be sufficient to confine ourselves to the report of the Conference on Faith and Order at Lund in 1952.

The report starts with a statement made at the Conference on Faith and Order at Edinburgh in 1937. "We regard sacramental intercommunion as a necessary part of any satisfactory church unity." In regard to the present possibility of intercommunion the report from Lund states: the majority of the churches represented "believe that there already exists among the members of the World Council of Churches such a fundamental unity as to justify, or indeed require, joint participation at the Lord's Table. . . . Others, without questioning the reality of our present unity, believe that fellowship in the Sacrament rightly exists only where there is fuller agreement in doctrine, a mutually acceptable ministry, or organic unity of church life." [1]

If we were to comment on these proposed conditions, we would have to say that the Eastern Orthodox church insists on all three, that the Anglicans would emphasize the second, and that some Lutherans would insist on the third. When a communion service was held in the cathedral in Lund during the conference, to which all delegates were invited, the members of the Eastern Orthodox church refused to attend, and so also did some Anglicans and a few German and American Lutherans. The reason given by the Lutherans was that the general invitation permitted some to attend who did not accept the Lutheran doctrine of the real presence.

The Eastern Orthodox church finds it difficult, even impossible, to use the term "intercommunion." According to their view the Lord's Supper is an act of the church as one body, and it cannot, therefore, be celebrated as an act of union between different "bodies." The whole question of intercommunion becomes from this point of view meaningless; the Lord's Supper can be celebrated only in an organically united church. The communion is not a means to achieve unity; rather, the common celebration is the result and the expression of a recovered unity. Consequently, G. Florovsky says that "the ecumenical movement is primarily a fellowship in search," [2] and another representative of the Eastern Orthodox church, L. Zander, says: "However high the partitions that divide Christians may be, they do not reach to heaven . . . and there, on high, the prayers that rise out of the depths of our separateness overcome those limitations and merge into one. Thus

---

[1] *Lund 1952*, p. 54.

[2] Donald M. Baillie and John Marsh (eds.), *Intercommunion*, the Report of the Theological Commission Appointed by the Continuation Committee of the World Conference on Faith and Order (New York: Harper, 1952), p 203. Cited hereafter as *Intercommunion*.

communio sanctorum makes up for the impossibility of *communicatio in sacris.*" [3]

Since Eastern Orthodox churchmen will not accept any communion fellowship which does not rest on an already achieved unity, they must take a passive attitude toward any attempt toward establishing intercommunion under present circumstances. They are not alone in holding that a common celebration of the eucharist should be an expression of re-established unity. Individual representatives of both Anglicans and Lutherans hold the same view. But in general this attitude does not exclude the possibility that a communion fellowship without complete organizational unity might be established. The report from Lund emphasizes that the question of intercommunion becomes more and more acute for the different denominations. It points out that a number of factors contribute toward a growing desire for communion fellowship, and that chief among these is the Lord's call to and his demand on his church. The report emphasizes both the necessity of doing without delay whatever can be done, and the importance of taking seriously the actual differences between the denominations. It is of utmost importance, they say, that unity shall be based on Scripture and be tested by conformity to the Word of God.[4] The conclusion strikes a characteristic note: "In closing this section of our report, we cannot but express our deep disappointment and concern that there is not a larger measure of agreement among us. We echo the view of the preparatory Commission on *Intercommunion* that 'neither we nor the Churches from which we come have yet gone deeply enough into the penitence from which healing may arise.' " [5]

The hindrances in the way of communion fellowship arise, as we have seen, both from questions of doctrine and from the development of church order. It is rightly pointed out, however, that

[3] *Ibid.,* p. 359.
[4] *Lund* 1952, p. 50.
[5] *Ibid.,* p. 57.

the elements of division must be seen in the perspective of the worship life and practice of each denomination. The character and form of the eucharistic service, for example, depends on the position taken in regard to the element of sacrifice. One form of the worship service which some regard as ideal may strike others as foreign and even repulsive. On the basis of the conversations held to date the impression prevails that the sharpest differences lie in the area of church order, since both the Eastern Orthodox and the Anglo-Catholic faction within the Church of England demand episcopal ordination on the basis of "apostolic succession" if the celebration of the eucharist is to be regarded as valid. Since it seems impossible for such a stand to receive universal endorsement, it might appear that here we stand before an insurmountable obstacle. Obviously we do not expect one denomination to capitulate to the other. We can make no progress in that direction. The conference in Lund, however, refused to regard the situation as hopeless. In this connection the conference made one of its most important statements. "We are agreed in recognising the administration of the Lord's Supper in the divided Churches, when controlled by the words of institution, as real means of grace through which Christ gives himself to those who in faith receive the appointed elements of bread and wine." [6]

If we now consider this discussion of intercommunion in principle, we must differentiate between the actual unity which is given in Holy Communion and the demonstration of this unity in practice which is expressed through our mutual participation at the communion table. I regard it as sufficient here to agree with the statement made by Bishop Anders Nygren. ". . . we must not exaggerate the extent of this [present] division. Even where two Church communions refuse the fellowship of the Lord's Supper to one another and believe themselves unable to meet with one another at the Lord's Table, they yet cannot dissolve the fellowship

[6] *Ibid.*, p. 53.

that exists in the fact that both—each for itself—partake of the one loaf: 'Because there is one loaf, we who are many are one body, for we all partake of the same loaf' (I Cor. 10:17). While coming together at the same table—which ought to be the Lord's Table and not that of an individual Communion—it can happen that one Communion will refuse Table fellowship with another. It cannot, however, prevent participation in the same bread. The given unity can never be nullified by any external division. The *skandalon* of Christendom consists, not in its lack of fellowship in Holy Communion, for this exists and can never be broken, but the lack of actualization of this fellowship in the life of the Church. That the unity exists, but that we ourselves retard and hinder it from actualization, this is our *skandalon.*" [7]

The statement about Holy Communion which the Conference in Edinburgh accepted after long preliminary studies has two parts: an introduction and an analysis. The analysis seeks to define the essential motifs of the Lord's Supper. The starting point is the agreement in regard to the presence of Christ. "We all believe that Christ is truly present in the eucharist, though as to how that presence is manifested and realized we may differ." They do not want to formulate any precise definition of the nature of his presence, since this would lead to divisive reservations. All attempts to impose definite formulations on the church have in the past become a cause of disunity. Obviously the significance of these statements is that "the real presence" is essential, but that no definite interpretation can be set up as a condition for the unity of the church. "The important thing is that we should celebrate the eucharist with the unfailing use of bread and wine, and of prayer, and of the words of institution, and with agreement as to its essential and spiritual meaning."

The conference elaborates on this spiritual meaning in this

[7] Anders Nygren, *Christ and His Church*, tr. by Alan Carlsten (Philadelphia: Westminster, 1956), pp. 122-23.

manner. "If sacrifice is understood as it was by our Lord and His followers and in the early Church, it includes, not His death only, but the obedience of His earthly ministry, and His risen and ascended life, in which He still does His Father's will and ever liveth to make intercession for us. Such a sacrifice can never be repeated, but is proclaimed and set forth in the eucharistic action of the whole Church when we come to God in Christ at the Eucharist or the Lord's Supper. For us, the secret of joining in that sacrifice is both the worship and the service of God; corporate because we are joined to Christ, and in Him to one another (I Cor. 10-17); individual, because each one of us makes the corporate act of self-oblation his own; and not ceremonial only, but also profoundly ethical, because the keynote of all sacrifice and offering is 'Lo! I come to do Thy will, O God.' We believe also that the Eucharist is a supreme moment of prayer, because the Lord is the celebrant or minister for us at every celebration, and it is in His prayers for God's gifts and for us all that we join. According to the New Testament accounts of the institution His prayer is itself a giving of thanks; so that the Lord's Supper is both a *verbum visibile* of the divine grace, and the supreme thanksgiving (*eucharistia*) of the people of God. We are throughout in the realm of the Spirit. It is through the Holy Spirit that the blessing and the gift are given. The presence, which we do not try to define, is a spiritual presence. We begin from the historical fact of the Incarnation in the power of the Holy Spirit, and we are already moving forward to the complete spiritual reality of the coming of the Lord and the life of the Heavenly City." [8]

In a note added to this statement the conference expresses its thanks to the Bishop of Lincoln, F. C. N. Hicks, for his exposition of the idea of sacrifice in the eucharist. His statement has strongly influenced the pronouncement made by the conference. The note

[8] Leonard Hodgson (ed.), *The Second World Conference on Faith and Order Held at Edinburgh 1937* (New York: Macmillan, 1938), p. 244f. Cited hereafter as *Edinburgh 1937*.

contains also a special statement by the representatives of the Eastern Orthodox church, in which it is maintained that the Holy Eucharist is an extension of the only and once-offered sacrifice of our Lord Jesus Christ, that the offered gifts are changed (*metaballontai*) into the very body and blood of our Lord Jesus Christ, and that the Holy Eucharist can be celebrated only by a validly ordained minister. Finally it is stated that certain other delegates would wish to make a somewhat similar statement.

When we analyze this statement by the Edinburgh Conference, it becomes obvious that the idea of sacrifice dominates the interpretation of the Lord's Supper. It should be noted, too, that the statements about sacrifice have been formulated in such a way that they could be accepted by several of the church bodies. In discussing the relation of the sacrifice of Christ to the eucharist they naturally repudiate the idea of a repetition of that sacrifice. The Eastern Orthodox use a word that can be variously interpreted, but it is quite certain that they would not speak of a repetition of the sacrifice made once for all. The conference statement emphasizes that the sacrifice of Christ does not refer exclusively to his death on the cross; the sacrifice that is "proclaimed and set forth" in the eucharistic action is a sacrifice that comprises the whole life of Christ from the incarnation to that life which the risen Lord lives in heaven. We encounter here a conception which has played a large part in the current ecumenical discussions about the Lord's Supper.

When later on they talk about the eucharist as our sacrifice, they associate this sacrifice with that of Christ. We participate in and join in his sacrifice. Our sacrifice is regarded from two points of view. On the one hand, it is worship, the church's highest form of thanksgiving (*eucharistia*), and, on the other hand, individual and corporate self-oblation in the service of God. Two factors are to be noted. First, it is not at all suggested that we in any way offer Christ; and second, the idea of fellowship is combined with the idea of sacrifice. We are able to bring our sacrifice of worship and service because "we are united with Christ and through Him with one another."

We may also note that the statement of the conference strongly emphasizes the character of the eucharist as "the supreme moment of prayer," and that this prayer is associated with the high priestly prayer of Christ. Finally we may remark that the eschatological aspect is present but not especially accentuated.

The discussion of the eucharist at the Conference in Lund was preceded by an exchange of views which resulted in the publication of two reports: *Intercommunion* and *Ways of Worship*. The Conference in Lund makes the following principal statement.

"Whatever may be our various opinions on the nature and efficacy of ritual acts, we are all agreed that *Deus non alligatur sacramentis,* and that (in the words of the Gospel) 'the wind bloweth where it listeth . . . so is everyone that is born of the Spirit' (John 3:8). We record in thanksgiving that we have reached in our discussions a measure of understanding, which none of us could have anticipated, on the problem of the sacrificial element in Holy Communion. The mystery of the love of God, which we celebrate at the Lord's Table, surpasses human expression. But in our attempts to describe that mystery we have the warrant of Holy Scripture for using sacrificial language. 'Behold the Lamb of God.' Our Lord Jesus Christ in all His life on earth and chiefly in His death and resurrection has overcome the powers of darkness. In His one perfect and sufficient sacrifice on Calvary He offered perfect obedience to the Father in atonement for the sin of the whole world. This was an act of expiation made once and for all and is unrepeatable. In His risen and ascended life He ever makes intercession for us.

"Our response in worship, then, is the praise, prayer, thanksgiving and offering of ourselves in faith and obedience made to the Father in the name of Jesus Christ. We make the sacrifice of praise and thanksgiving. It is at this point that our greatest difficulties arise as we seek to express just how our worship on earth is related to the eternal intercession of Christ in heaven. We all agree that there is an element of mystery here which can scarcely be expressed (Rom. 8:26).

"Some of us believe that in the Lord's Supper, where they enter into communion with the crucified and risen Lord, they only offer a sacrifice of praise and thanksgiving and obedient service as a response in faith to the benefits the Lord gives us. Others would like to insist, however, that in the Holy Eucharist the Lord Jesus Christ as God's Great High Priest unites the oblation made by His body, the Church, with His own sacrifice, and so takes up her own adoration into the *Sanctus* of the company of heaven. Between these two views there are others to which a brief reference may not do full justice.

"It is felt, however, that a deeper understanding of the meaning of 'unites' in the above paragraph, particularly in the light of biblical eschatology, might help to resolve real divergence and misunderstanding at this point." [9]

In a note we are told that some delegates were disappointed that the idea of sacrifice and not the real presence has become the central element in the discussion of the Lord's Supper.

We may quote here an additional statement about the significance of the Lord's Supper. "This dominical sacrament of Christ's Body and Blood . . . is (a) a memorial of Christ's incarnation and earthly ministry, of his death and resurrection; (b) a sacrament in which He is truly present to give Himself to us, uniting us to Himself, to His eternal sacrifice, and to one another; and (c) eschatologically, an anticipation of our fellowship with Christ in His eternal kingdom." [10]

When we compare these statements with that made by the

[9] *Lund 1952*, p. 42f.
[10] *Ibid.*, p. 53f.

Edinburgh Conference, we find that the emphasis on sacrifice appears more strongly than before. The Lund Conference dealt so exclusively with this problem that some felt it necessary to deplore this one-sided emphasis. It seems that some of the Lutherans would insist on a more thoroughgoing discussion of the real presence.

The assertion that we have attained to an unexpected consensus of opinion in regard to the element of sacrifice in the eucharist is rather surprising. We need not question the correctness of this statement. But it is perplexing that in the statement which follows there is nothing to indicate in what this growing agreement consists. The presentation of the common point of view does not advance beyond the statement made in Edinburgh, rather the opposite. In contrast to Edinburgh the Lund Conference defines the antitheses which stand over against one another in regard to sacrifice. The report distinguishes between two main antitheses, and declares also that there are other points of view which would appear somewhere between these two extremes. But the brief statements in the Lund document do not clarify the nature of these antitheses, nor indicate the motives behind them. In order to arrive at a clear understanding it is necessary to examine the preliminary studies made in preparation for the conference, especially the two volumes: *Intercommunion* and *Ways of Worship*.

Before we leave the Lund Conference report we may note that it suggests that a biblical-exegetical orientation, with special attention given to the eschatological perspective, might help to further ecumenical conversations and remove misunderstandings and conflicts. This statement is characteristic of the conference. Similar suggestions were made in other connections. These ideas are in line with tendencies which have become strong in the more recent ecumenical discussions.

2

Voices from Various Church Communions

We are concerned in this chapter with the discussions which preceded the Lund Conference, and which resulted in the two composite works: *Intercommunion* and *Ways of Worship*. Can we find anything here which will help to explain the statement of the conference about an unexpected agreement in regard to the sacrificial element in the eucharist? Or let us put the question thus: do we find in these preliminary documents any signs of such a growing agreement? It is not surprising that in general the authors seem to have agreed on the Lord's Supper as "a sacrifice of thanksgiving" (*eucharistia*), and that they combine our sacrifice of willing service with the communion. Both of these points have frequently been obscured. But they do not in themselves involve a controversial element, and they ought not, therefore, to have caused disagreements in ecumenical discussions. The problem of the relationship between the sacrifice of Christ and the Lord's Supper is a very different matter. Here we encounter a highly controversial subject. Our interest, therefore, is directed primarily to what the representatives of the various churches have to say on this matter.

We shall examine first the presentations made by representatives of the Eastern Orthodox church. We do not find here any extensive explanation of their conception of Holy Communion as a sacrifice. But they point out very clearly that agreement in doctrine is an essential presupposition for communion fellowship, and that the conception of the Lord's Supper as a sacrifice belongs to this agreement. G. Florovsky states in an article, "Confessional Loyalty in the Ecumenical Movement," [1] that communion fellowship with anyone who regards the sacrifice of the mass as corruption and heresy is inconceivable. L. Zander expresses himself in similar terms in an article on "Intercommunion and Co-celebration" in *Intercommunion*.[2] By his participation in the eucharist the Eastern Orthodox Christian confesses the faith of the church and of the fathers, "but for a man who denies the sacrificial character of the Eucharist, does not revere Our Lady, has lost touch with the saints and believes that the consecrated elements are merely bread and wine, participation in an Orthodox Eucharist would be a falsehood, an outward sign without inner meaning, and, indeed, a betrayal of his own faith and disloyalty to his church."

The only Eastern Orthodox author who analyzes the sacrificial nature of the eucharist is L. Gillet.[3] He quotes a Greek theologian, Androutsos, as an authority. The eucharist is not a new sacrifice separated from the sacrifice on Golgotha in content and effect, but a new representation before God of the sacrifice made once and for all, and a new, mystical reiteration of it; a new presentation of the one and final sacrifice. We make no attempt here to interpret this statement. It is clear, however, that it represents a different point of view from that which characterized the medieval sacrifice of the mass.

We must now listen to a representative of the Old Catholics. A. E. Rüthy presents a very carefully formulated statement.[4] "Sacrifice in a Christian sense can only mean the sacrifice of God's Son on the Cross. Beside His, no sacrifice has any value in itself. The sacrifice of Christ was made once for all, and needs no comple-

[1] *Intercommunion*, p. 196ff.
[2] *Ibid.*, p. 352.
[3] Pehr Edwall, *et al.* (eds.), *Ways of Worship: The Report of a Theological Commission of Faith and Order* (New York: Harper, 1951), p. 184ff. Hereafter cited as *Ways of Worship*.
[4] *Ibid.*, p. 252.

tion or repetition, and it is effectual henceforth for believers throughout time. This continuous efficacy of the sacrifice on the Cross is represented in the church by the celebration of the Holy Eucharist. By receiving Holy Communion every believer is assured that Christ died for him too."

There are no documents which have dealt so thoroughly with the element of sacrifice as those produced by the Anglicans. A partial reason for this is no doubt the fact that we are dealing here with a question which has been the object of controversy within Anglicanism. A. H. Couratin reminds us in an article[5] that there are three very different traditions within the church of England. 1) The tradition from the time of the Reformation which rejected the idea of sacrifice except as the self-oblation of the communicants. 2) The tradition from the seventeenth century which agreed with the contemporary theologians who emphasized the real presence but rejected their idea of the eucharist as a re-presentative sacrifice. 3) The tradition from nineteenth-century tractarianism which spoke of the eucharist as a real atoning sacrifice for the living and the dead.

The chief reason why these Anglican authors devote so much study to the idea of sacrifice is their conviction that this is important for the ecumenical conversations. They take this attitude, not only on the basis of the insights gained in facing their own problems, but because they desire to base their interpretation of the eucharist on the Bible and the church fathers. From this starting point they claim to be able to present a balanced evaluation of the antitheses which originated in the Reformation. These Anglican scholars are willing to admit that much of the criticism of the eucharistic doctrine and practice of the later Medieval church was valid, but they maintain that this criticism was negatively dependent on the conceptions which the Reformers criticized, and that the interpretation of the eucharist by the Reformers, therefore, lost certain

[5] *Ibid.*, p. 188ff.

common, "catholic" values. This applies especially to the loss of the element of sacrifice.

It cannot be denied that the Anglican contributions have been extremely important in the ecumenical discussions of the Lord's Supper. Both the formulations of the problems and the declarations of the conferences have been strongly influenced by these studies. It will be necessary, therefore, to devote a chapter to a study and an analysis of the most important Anglican documents.

The Lutheran contributions to the preliminary studies do not deal extensively with the old controversies. They reveal, however, a positive interest in the idea of sacrifice. W. Stählin reminds us that the Lutheran confessions do not eliminate the sacrificial idea, and that especially the Apology to the Augsburg Confession strongly emphasizes the Holy Communion as a sacrifice of thanksgiving, while it rejects the idea of an atoning sacrifice. He points out that Luther's exclusion of everything relating to sacrifice in the German Mass (1526) had far-reaching consequences.[6] "Since then the Lutheran Church has shown an almost ineradicable suspicion concerning the very idea of sacrifice in the Eucharist, for fear that the emphasis on man's sacrificial activity might obscure the exclusiveness of the divine gift of grace which we human beings can only gratefully receive and accept. In present discussions amongst Lutheran theologians in Germany there are not a few who demand the re-institution of sacrifice to its due place within Christian worship. . . . Is it permissible to extend the necessary objection against a sub-Christian concept of sacrifice to the length of actually renouncing a term which is so strongly emphasized in biblical language?"

The Alsace theologian, R. Will, deals especially with the relationship between Word and sacrament, and finds evidence of a growing convergence between the various churches, both Roman and Protestant. The tendency is to reject the exclusiveness which

[6] *Ibid.,* p. 212f.

emphasizes the Word at the expense of the sacraments, and vice versa. Reports from many sources testify to the existence of such a centripetal tendency." [7]

We may add in this connection that the interest in a more positive attitude toward the idea of sacrifice, which Stählin claims to have found in modern German discussions, may be found in other areas of the Lutheran church. The Danish theologian, Regin Prenter, states rather emphatically in his dogmatics that the eucharist is the eternal presence in the church of the sacrifice on Golgotha. I will return to his statement later. Yngve Brilioth writes in *Eucharistic Faith and Practice:* "In Luther's day controversial needs rendered it impossible that he should allow any place to the Memorial-aspect. But the case is different now; today the enemy is no longer the Roman canon and the abuses that followed in its train, but rather the impoverishment of faith and of worship. The church of today has no grounds for refusing a place to this side of the Eucharist; rather she needs to aim at recovering the evangelical conception of the sacrament in its completeness, and drawing out the implications of Luther's own teaching and old Lutheran practice." [8]

The Reformed contributions in the preliminary studies to the Lund Conference are very interesting. This is especially true of the articles by the Dutch theologian, G. van der Leeuw and the Scottish theologian, T. F. Torrance. G. van der Leeuw was the chairman of the commission which edited the volume, *Ways of Worship,* but died before its publication. He maintains that the Reformed church is returning to a "sacramental realism" in accordance with the deepest intentions of this church. The designation of the sacraments as symbols and signs can be, and often has been, interpreted superficially, and the so-called spiritual interpretation has often come very close to heresy. The word "sign" must be

[7] *Ibid.,* p. 222f.
[8] Yngve Brilioth, *Eucharistic Faith and Practice,* tr. by A. G. Hebert (New York: Macmillan, 1931), p. 140.

used in its original, biblical, and apostolic meaning. It implies then, not only an indication or affirmation, but an action of God in the sacrament. This position rejects both transubstantiation and superficial symbolism, both of which are a form of rationalization.

From this point of view Van der Leeuw discusses the idea of sacrifice in the Lord's Supper.[9] "The idea of re-presentation as it is advocated in many circles nowadays, Roman Catholic as well as Anglican and Lutheran, seems to present some perspectives for a future development of sacramental theology for the Reformed Churches also. The central Sacrament, the Eucharist, is not a repetition of Christ's sacrifice, neither is it a making mention of it in a solemn way. But it is the re-presentation of the Act of God on Golgotha. By our humble means God is offering to us the sacrifice of His Son, presenting it to us. *Benedictus qui venit in nomine Domini* is no ornate phrase but a blissful reality: Christ suffering, Christ risen is coming ever anew to meet and to bless us."

We may observe that when Van der Leeuw uses the term re-presentation, he connects it with God's own action, and as a result emphasizes that the Christ who meets us in the eucharist is not only the crucified but also the risen Lord. He emphasizes the latter in contrast to the Pietistic interpretation which places the whole emphasis on the death of Christ. The conception of the sacrament as a repetition of the sacrifice on Golgotha, which even Roman theologians admit is an abomination, must not be allowed to discredit the idea of sacrifice itself. "At the Lord's Table the sacrifice of Christ is re-presented and the faithful are called upon to partake of this sacrifice. They cannot receive it and make it their own without giving themselves, without offering up their lives. At the Table of the Lord they are not only receivers of the gifts of Christ, but they officiate, they partake, they exercise the priesthood conferred upon them by Baptism and Confirmation." Van der Leeuw concludes by saying that these questions have been

[9] *Ways of Worship*, p. 229

discussed with growing interest during the past twenty-five years, that they have become since the war a primary concern of the church, and that out of these discussions there emerges now "a real theology."

Two contributions by Reformed theologians from Switzerland, A. Graf (German) and R. Paquier (French), present a vivid picture of the modest place accorded to the Lord's Supper and the inadequate conception of it that has prevailed in the church. Both of these articles, however, present a critical analysis of the situation and insist on a more adequate conception which will regard the Lord's Supper, not only as a memorial, but will restore to anamnesis the rich content it had in the ancient church. Graf writes: "The Church does not simply remember the death of the Lord: she 'represents' the sacrifice itself, letting herself enter into the suffering and death of Christ, into His obedience. In that way she proclaims His death 'until he come.'" [10]

Paquier discusses the liturgical renewal which has taken place in the French-speaking part of Switzerland during recent years, and offers the following comment: "However, it is only in elucidating the relation of the Word to the Sacrament, and in discriminating between symbol and sacrament, that a solid foundation will be assured for the laudable efforts made during the last few years in the Reformed Churches of French-speaking Switzerland to restore the sacraments to their proper place and value in the worship of the church." [11]

Among the Reformed contributions the article on "Eschatology and the Eucharist" by T. F. Torrance is well worth our attention. Here we find the most elaborate and clearest presentation of the idea of sacrifice in the Lord's Supper from the Reformed point of view. [12]

By way of introduction Torrance notes that in recent times the

[10] Ibid., p. 239.
[11] Ibid., p. 245.
[12] Intercommunion, pp. 301-360.

difference between Roman and evangelical teachings on the Lord's Supper has narrowed considerably. He reminds us of the revisions which a number of Roman theologians, beginning with Maurice de la Taille, have made. These Roman theologians have not been unmindful of the Protestant criticisms of the doctrine of the mass. Behind the shift which has taken place lies a new understanding of the biblical point of view and a rediscovery of the eschatological character of the sacrament. Nevertheless the difference between Roman and evangelical views is very deep, much deeper than between the various branches of the evangelical churches.

The intention of Torrance is to develop a more profound view of the Lord's Supper on a biblical and eschatological basis. We can refer here only to the chief points in his presentation of the idea of sacrifice. According to Torrance the sacrament is a combination of divine and human action. It is a divine action of *totus Christus,* the divine Man, the Christ incarnate. The action of Christ and the re-action of the church are combined in the Lord's Supper. These two actions can be neither identified nor separated. When Jesus gave his disciples the broken bread and the cup of wine at the last meal, he associated them with his sacrifice and constituted them as the church concorporate with himself. "Through the Eucharist the Church becomes, so to speak, the great arch that spans history, supported by only two pillars, the cross which stands on this side of time, and the coming of Christ in power which stands at the end of history." As the church militant in this world it participates both in the agony of Golgotha and in the triumph of the Savior.

The Lord's Supper as a memorial is an anamnesis both before God and before man, and the same is true of the Lord's Supper as a proclamation of the death of Christ until he comes. Anamnesis is both historical and eternal. It is a memorial of the death and resurrection, both of which "through the eternal Spirit" become a present reality. But this anamnesis of the atoning death of Christ and its eternal power includes eucharistic intercession. The sacramental memory expresses itself inevitably in prayer, the prayer that clings to the cross of Christ and holds it up before the Father. It is a prayer in which the Spirit himself prays for us, and as such it is an echo in the church of the intercessory prayer of the great High Priest. Through the anamnesis the church enters into the passion of the Redeemer, and in his name travails in prayer for all mankind.

The proclamation of the death of Jesus has the same sacramental character. The eucharistic proclamation "enshrines as its eternal *canto firma* the Self-consecration of the Lamb of God, the Self-presentation of the Mediator before the face of the Father in His Intercession for the Church, but this is the *mysterion* which is the dimension in infinite depth behind the action of the Church in the Lord's Supper." The profound mystery of Holy Communion is that the church is permitted to participate (*koinonein*) in Christ's substitutionary Self-consecration (John 17). In reality it is the risen Lord himself who is the true celebrant at the holy Table. If this were not true, the eucharistic sacrifice would become but a pagan ceremony. The church's *re-actio* partakes of sacrificial character, but if *re-actio* becomes identified with *actio,* the sacrament is destroyed because its derivative, sacramental, and analogical nature is denied. "It is clear, therefore, that the bringing of the Eucharist under the rubric of proclamation excludes the idea of its being a sacrifice in itself or in its own right. . . . The Eucharist is the sacramental counterpart to the unique sacrifice of Christ, and therefore in its own way, inasmuch as it echoes that, and is derivative from it, a sacramental sacrifice." In reality it is Christ who in the eucharist represents to the church and makes effective for the church his own atoning deed of sacrifice.

In this connection Torrance enters on a discussion of the important problem of the relationship between the Lord's Supper and the atonement. The interpretation of the Lord's Supper and the eucharistic sacrifice depends on the significance of the atonement. The eucharistic proclamation points to the divine action as the heart of it all. It does so because the divine action is the mystery of the atonement: God gave his only-begotten and beloved Son as a sacrifice, and the atoning deed is his and his alone. Theologians of "the Catholic type" often miss this most crucial point when they use "sacrifice" and "offering" univocally of God and of the church. In reality the word sacrifice must in this connection be given different meanings. The eucharistic sacrifice is different from the atoning sacrifice of Christ. Our sacrifice is subordinated under his unique sacrifice which was made once for all and is eternally effective. The uniqueness of his sacrifice consists both in his bearing God's judgment on man's sin and in his perfect obedience. In both of these respects Christ stood alone. In his vicarious deed of atonement he did what we cannot do. He did it in our stead, for us and as our deed. Our answer in the eucharistic sacrifice may be regarded as "the counter-sacrifice of the Church, but never can it be said to be of the same genus as the unique sacrifice of Christ Himself. By participation in His body and blood He permits us to be associated with His sacrifice, but in such a way, as in the Garden of Gethsemane, that He removes Himself to a holy distance from us. We may indeed watch with Him, but in the awful hour of His agony we know that He dies alone and we are found among those who crucify Him. What makes Christ's sacrifice absolutely unique is the identity between the Offerer and the Offering and Him to whom the Offering is made. . . . It is that identity which sets His sacrifice absolutely apart from anything else, and makes it quite clear that the eucharistic sacrifice is only the *anamnesis* or *proclamation* of that lonely sacrifice, and does not involve any identity between a sacrifice of our own and His."

In concluding his presentation of the idea of sacrifice in the Lord's Supper Torrance emphasizes the necessity of understanding the atonement as an act of God. If this is not done, it results in false conceptions of sacrifice. But the atonement as an act of God does not imply that the humanity of Christ becomes obscured. "It was not the Godhead *qua* Godhead that atoned, it was the God-manhood." It was not God *in* man, but God *as* man. The manhood was essential and not merely instrumental. The atonement is, therefore, in the real sense of the word substitutionary. Torrance wants to uphold the truth which, he says, is contained in the statement that the eucharistic sacrifice presents the sacrifice of Christ before the Father. But such a statement must not be interpreted to mean that the atonement is not altogether a divine act. "Once it is clearly seen, however, that the atonement is God's act, and that He bears in Himself our judgment, that He does in Jesus what we cannot do, then the false doctrine of identity falls to the ground, and a true doctrine of the Eucharist can be enunciated."

Finally we note a couple of Baptist documents. V. E. Devadutt of India writes: [13] The Lord himself is the host at his Table, he who gave his life a ransom for many. The feast was instituted by the Lord in order that his followers should not forget his death for sinners. "If it was instituted with that urgent purpose, may there not be in the Feast something more than of a mere memorial significance? May it not be an occasion in a real sense for the participant in the Feast to enter into fellowship with the sufferings of Christ? There is something 'objective' here which cannot be defined—perhaps it is better not defined. Some of the hymns we sing seem to bring this out more clearly than our theological formulations."

An English Baptist, P. W. Evans,[14] maintains that the criticism of the conception of the Lord's Supper held by members of the "free churches" very often rests on ignorance. That is true when it is asserted that the Baptists regard the Feast merely as a memorial. The bread and wine are for many Christians, even if they

[13] *Ibid.*, p. 178ff.
[14] *Ibid.*, p. 185ff.

may not go further, so sacred that little beseems any other Christians to mock at the meaning they attach to it. No Christian communion finds in the Lord's Supper anything *less* than a proclamation of the death of Christ until he comes. The view criticised therefore is not erroneous, though defective, and the question arises whether "a defective understanding of the full meaning of the Sacrament prevents it from being a means of grace to the sincere communicant."

As a complement to these last presentations I refer also to a statement in the report which a number of English free churchmen presented to the Archbishop of Canterbury under the title: *The Catholicity of Protestantism*. "The Lord's Supper is not merely a solemn memorial of Christ's sacrifice of himself, the sacrifice which was once offered on the cross. The Lord's Supper is the dramatic setting forth of this sacrifice, and the means through which we can participate in it and in all its benefits. Because in the sacrament the crucified and risen Savior is himself present to share with us all that is his." [15]

When we look back at these statements by various church communions on the idea of sacrifice in the Lord's Supper, we must note that the positive interest is obvious and surprisingly strong. It is clear that, at least to some extent, there were reasons for the assertion made by the Lund Conference that "we have reached in our discussion a measure of understanding, which none of us could have anticipated, on the problem of the sacrificial element in Holy Communion." It is obvious that there were also reasons for registering different points of view. Our review of these presentations raises many questions which demand that we define our attitude to them. But before we enter on an analysis of these problems we must take note of those Anglican documents which more than any others have actualized and defined the discussion.

[15] R. Newton Flew and Rupert E. Davies (eds.), *The Catholicity of Protestantism* (Philadelphia: Muhlenberg, 1951), p. 112.

3

Some Anglican Documents

The Conference in Edinburgh decided that a memorandum prepared by Bishop Hicks should be printed as an appendix to the
report of the conference.[1] This action indicates how much significance was attached to this document. A comparison between the
conference report and the main points in Hicks' memorandum
indicates to what extent the latter influenced the formulations of
the final report.

The main purpose of Hicks' presentation is, on the one hand,
to make clear how the idea of sacrifice became misinterpreted in
the Medieval tradition and what was legitimate in the criticism
made by the Reformation; and, on the other hand, to present a
conception of sacrifice which is biblically sound, and therefore able
to solve in a positive manner the problems with which the Reformers struggled.

Hicks points out first of all that already through the words of
institution the idea of sacrifice was connected with the eucharist,
and that the fathers in the ancient church used sacrificial language
when they discussed the Lord's Supper. Later when the Medieval
theologians began to speculate concerning the kind of sacrifice
made in the mass, they had no conception of the Jewish background of the ideas of sacrifice in the ancient church. The result
was the assumption that sacrifice consists solely in the death of
the victim. The sacrifice in the eucharist became in some sense

[1] *Edinburgh 1937*, p. 325ff.

a repetition of the death on Golgotha. Against this the protest of the Reformers was justified. They emphasized the uniqueness and all-sufficiency of the sacrifice made once for all, but in doing so they also abandoned the agelong association of sacrifice with the eucharist. The Medieval conception of the sacrifice of the mass resulted also in the belief that what is offered in the eucharistic elements is the same body which was offered on Golgotha. In popular understanding, at any rate, the conception of the real presence became material and carnal. If this was what the real presence meant, the Reformers could not but modify it, explain it away, or deny it. They looked with suspicion on or denied both the sacrifice and the real presence. The Western "Catholics," however, remained loyal to the tradition as they understood it.

It was not possible to escape from this deadlock until we had learned what sacrifice signified in the Old Testament and consequently what constituted the background of the thinking in the ancient church. Hicks emphasizes that according to the Old Testament conception the death of the victim was but the first stage in the sacrifice as a whole. In his presentation of the sacrifice of Christ Hicks proceeds from the incarnation. The Lord makes himself one with us in his incarnation. We crucify him. He, our High Priest, takes his blood, his life, which by the power of the incarnation is our life, and brings it through the veil into the very presence of God. He atones for us. His manhood is offered to God in eternal service, and as God accepts this offering, he transforms it. Through his resurrection and ascension the body of his humiliation becomes spiritual, heavenly, glorified.

Hicks regards it as of decisive importance that the sacrifice of Christ is continuous. He is still obedient as he sits on the right hand of the Father, for he is still man. But now he does not obey alone. We, the church, obey in him. When we "offer him," we offer ourselves, our souls and bodies. Our offering is received and transformed. It is imperfect, and therefore we can offer it only in union with the whole body whose Head is Christ. So we offer ourselves in him, for his merits, and him for us. This our offering results in communion. The communion presupposes the offering, but the offering is incomplete and meaningless without the communion.

On the basis of this discussion Hicks draws the following two conclusions. In the first place, there can be no sort of repetition of his sacrifice in the eucharist, no taking away from the uniqueness and all-sufficiency of the cross. In the second place, there can be no idea of anything materialistic in the presence. The presence is true and real because it is spiritual, but it is not spiritual in a negative sense because it is a mystery in which by the power of the Spirit earth and heaven, earthly and heavenly things, are united. We are lifted up into heaven and admitted to the heavenly worship which the Book of Revelation describes in chapters 4-7.

On the basis of this point of view Hicks considers that the criticism by the Reformers has been accorded its relative merit, and at the same time the idea of sacrifice has been established as legitimate, and thus the reasons for the criticism have been removed.

Toward the close of the memorandum Hicks speaks of the Lord's Supper as a eucharist. The point of departure is in the words of thanksgiving and blessing which Jesus spoke on the last evening and which we call his "consecration prayer," while "the words of institution" might with better reason be called "words of administration." The sacrifice in the Lord's Supper is fully united with thanksgiving and prayer. He continually lives and prays for us. Only through his prayer and his perfect sacrifice do our prayers have any value. The eucharist is the supreme moment of our prayer. The whole eucharist, and especially that which is called consecration, is effective prayer. "There can be no magic in it. We ask for God's greatest gift, Himself, and because our Lord is the celebrant of every earthly Eucharist, it is He who asks; and to

the prevailing prayer of, and the fulness of the inevitable answer
to, His thanksgiving prayer there can be no limit."

As we have already stated the memorandum by Bishop Hicks
played a very significant part at the conference in Edinburgh. Not
only the chief points stated in the report of the conference, but
also the formulation of these points, depend on this document.
We receive the impression that the delegates were overwhelmed
by the arguments presented, and that the resultant unity was far
less substantial than it appeared. In any case the conference in
Lund, in spite of its expressed surprise at the measure of consensus
in regard to the sacrificial element in the Lord's Supper, has reg-
istered differences which in reality touch upon points on which
the delegates in Edinburgh were supposed to have agreed on the
basis of Hicks' statement.

We may for the present postpone the questions and comments
which arise on the basis of Hicks' memorandum, especially since
many of his ideas recur in other Anglican documents. This is true
both of the emphasis on the continuation of the sacrifice of Christ
in heaven and of the statement that in the eucharist we "offer
Christ."

A. G. Hebert has given his article in *Intercommunion,* dealing
with the idea of sacrifice in the Lord's Supper, the title: "A Root
of Difference and Unity." [2] Hebert is convinced that it is now possible to overcome the sharp antitheses within Christendom which
have characterized especially the discussion of the idea of sacrifice
in the Lord's Supper. He states that his purpose is to help "protestant" Christians to a living sympathy with "catholic" Christians,
not only those who participate in the ecumenical movement, but
also Roman Catholics who at present are prevented from attend-
ing, but who follow the procedure with deep interest and prayer.
Hebert grants without reservation the legitimacy of the Reformation opposition to the Medieval errors. But at the same time he

[2] *Intercommunion,* p. 236ff.

maintains that something essential was lost: the "central" idea of sacrifice, "the eucharistic sacrifice." This idea of sacrifice, however, may be so interpreted that it does not conflict with the ideas represented by the Reformers. Not only that, but Hebert intends to show that the sacrifice in the Lord's Supper, as he interprets it, is directly compatible with the Pauline-Lutheran doctrine of justification by faith, with its *sola fide—sola gratia,* and strictly speaking, is a necessary consequence of this doctrine.

As Anglicans usually do, Hebert starts with the difference between a "catholic" and a "protestant" type. Such a portrayal is usually precarious. Protestants find it difficult to recognize themselves in the picture. Furthermore, it might be questioned whether it is possible to draw a coherent picture of anything so heterogeneous as the Protestant denominations. It seems to be true, too, that the Catholics are just as little satisfied with what the Protestants say about "the catholic type." It may also happen that Roman Catholics and Anglicans have different ideas about what is really catholic. It would be in the interest of furthering the ecumenical work if we would cease to classify and describe these types, since in many instances it becomes misleading.

However, according to Hebert, the sermon is the supreme point of worship for the Protestant. Here he encounters God's living and saving Word. The same divine gift is mediated also in a different form in the sacraments. In both cases it is a movement from God to man, and man's part is essentially receptive. There is indeed a Godward movement on man's part, but this is the work of the Spirit, and can therefore not be formalized in fixed liturgical rites. This must be left to the individual, although it may find spontaneous expressions in hymns of praise. For the Catholic, on the contrary, the supreme moment of worship is the offering of Christ's own sacrifice and the unity of his people with him in the communion. Here, too, there is a manward movement, the gift of salvation, but this is completed in the Godward movement of liturgical prayers, praise, and adoration through Jesus Christ our Lord.

The question about the eucharistic sacrifice has been a storm center. This whole complex of ideas has been violently attacked by Protestants because it seems to imply that we are able to propitiate God by the sacrifices that we make, and that thereby Christ has, as it were, put himself into our hands. There has been much in Catholic doctrine and practice that justifies the protest, and it cannot be maintained that there is no longer any cause for opposition. But a modern, more accurate biblical study has provided new possibilities of better understanding of the matter, and enables us to present a doctrine of the eucharistic sacrifice which is truly "evangelical." Hebert refers to Hicks' book, *The Fulness of Sacrifice,* of which the memorandum presented at Edinburgh was a digest, and also to a book by the Roman theologian, E. Masure, *Le Sacrifice du Chef* (1932), in an English translation entitled *The Christian Sacrifice* (1943).

After a review of the ideas of sacrifice in the Old Testament Hebert asserts that the purpose and significance of sacrifice have been fulfilled in Christ and his church. When Jesus instituted the Lord's Supper, he interpreted his death as a sacrifice, and this interpretation is echoed in manifold ways in the New Testament witness to his sacrificial death. This is the Sacrifice, of which the Old Testament ritual was a type and a shadow. We must also observe that, according to the New Testament, those who participate in the worship do so not only as spectators at a sacrifice. They themselves are included in the offering; their lives are offered up in union with Christ as a reasonable, holy, and living sacrifice (Rom. 12:1; cf. Rom. 15:16).

On the basis of Hebrews 10:19-22 Hebert emphasizes the permanence of Christ's act of sacrifice. Our High Priest continually offers his sacrifice at the heavenly altar. The author of the Letter to the Hebrews calls us to join in sacrificial worship with the ascended Christ. We are not to immolate Christ over again, nor to offer some sacrifice in addition to his sacrifice. What is intended is that we shall join as participants in the one sacrifice which Christ makes at the heavenly altar. The Lord's Supper has been celebrated repeatedly in various places throughout the centuries. But there is no multiplicity in the sacrifice itself. It is one, and therefore it is the meeting place of the whole universal church, those whom we call "living" on earth, and the faithful departed, and the saints in heaven. Thus we are united in common worship and prayer with the whole family of God. What happens is not that a group of individual people meet in order that each one may conduct his own private worship, but rather that the individuals come to join in praise, meditation, and supplication with the whole body of Christ.

There was much, however, in the Lord's Supper which could be misinterpreted and corrupted. At the close of the Middle Ages there was an abundance of such perversions. The supreme disaster was the elimination of the communion of the people from the great Sunday eucharist. The congregation became onlookers at a rite performed by the clergy in the sanctuary. The elevation of the Host became now the center of the rite. Theology became concentrated on transubstantiation. Difficulties were encountered in the theological explanation of the sacrifice, and they were rendered insoluble by the mistake of treating the immolation as the central point in the sacrifice. It was assumed that Christ was somehow "mystically" re-immolated and that the Lord's Supper was a new sacrifice. The paid chantry masses increased enormously, and prayers for the dead and the cult of the saints dropped to what was in fact a pagan level.

It is not surprising that the Reformation acted drastically. The positive contribution of the Reformation, according to Hebert, was, on the one hand, that the communion of the people became again an integral part of the eucharistic action, and, on the other hand, that the celebration of the eucharist was an act of the assembled church, and not the act primarily of the individual priest. But these points were gained at the cost of the idea of the eucharistic sacrifice. The words of the Letter to the Hebrews concerning the ministry of Christ at the heavenly altar, which Luther had noted, did not lead to a positive conception of the eucharistic sacrifice. The reason for this was that the offering of Christ continued to be identified with his death, with the immolation. The result was that the Protestant interpretation of the Lord's Supper became concentrated in the communion in which Christ bestows forgiveness of sin on the believers. This gift was then understood, "especially by the Lutherans," in the largest sense as embracing the whole work of grace and as including the gift of salvation and deliverance, joy and peace. The intention of Luther and of the Anglican reformers, and the expressed desire of Calvin, that the communion service should form the climax of each Sunday morning's worship was not realized. The regular Protestant type of Sunday worship became a nonsacrificial service.

Hebert intends in his own presentation to preserve the two positive contributions of the Reformation and to combine with them a new conception of the eucharistic sacrifice. He maintains that there is no incongruity, but an essential unity, between the Pauline thesis of justification by faith and the idea of the eucharistic sacrifice. To be justified by faith means to be justified by God's grace through the redemption that is in Christ Jesus (Rom. 3:24). Faith is not a meritorious work, but the reception of God's grace in Christ, whom God has set forth as an expiation (Rom. 3:25). "God has saved us; we are not able to save ourselves. Here is the Christian doctrine of salvation; and it is divinely simple. Yet that which is in itself simple is very easily misunderstood and perverted by us, for we are not simple."

The eucharistic sacrifice, says Hebert, is in itself simple, with this same sort of simplicity. He interprets this theme in the following manner. I want to pray for someone. But how can I expect that God will receive my weak and uncertain prayer? If I prayed better, might I then expect that God would receive my prayer because of its quality? No, but I take it along to the altar and offer it in the eucharist. There I hold up before God Christ's own sacrifice, Christ's love for the person I am praying for, Christ's death for his salvation. I do not bring to God my devout apprehension of the love which Christ has for this person, but that love itself as it objectively exists in the prayer which Christ makes, and as it objectively exists in the sacrament which he has given us. All claim to personal merit on my part is excluded.

Hebert finds it paradoxical that the Reformation principle of justification by faith seems to be bound up with the "offering" of Christ which the Reformers vigorously attacked. He is opposed to those who hold that our offering in the eucharist can consist only in our offering of ourselves and of our thanksgiving, and who justify this view by saying that Christ's offering is an offer which he alone can make. It is true, says Hebert, that the eucharistic sacrifice is indeed Christ's own sacrifice, and that he is the real celebrant. Yet there is an action in the Lord's Supper which we do. We assemble, make our Offertory, we consecrate and receive. All this is an act of offering which derives its significance from the action which our Lord performed on the night of his passion. "We took the elements which He commanded, and used His words: with them we offered His Sacrifice, as participants in His Sacrifice at the heavenly altar, and that action was the sign and means of our justification by faith in Him; and in that action we ourselves were offered up to be a living sacrifice." [3]

Even though Hebert has emphasized how simple the conception of the eucharistic sacrifice really is, he now tells us that this is an action which can be expressed only in paradoxes and contradictory phrases. We perform an action; it is a sacrificial action, and the

[3] *Ibid.*, p. 250.

sacrifice that we offer is Christ's own sacrifice. Yet, in the reality signified by the sign, it is he who here offers his own sacrifice. The Lord's Supper is something more than a human commemoration of his passion. It is of the nature of a sacrament that the thing signified is present in the sign, and in the eucharist the action that we perform is the offering of Christ's sacrifice. It is really misleading to say that the only offering which we make is the sacrifice of ourselves. This notion leads back along the false road which makes the eucharistic offering an offering of *ours*. The offering of ourselves signifies, as Hebert has said in another connection, that we offer our insufficiency and our need; we have in reality nothing else to offer.

When we examine Hebert's presentation of the idea of the eucharistic sacrifice, we realize that we have here a document which is not only interesting as an expression of modern Anglicanism, but also important for ecumenical discussions. No one can deny that Hebert comes to his task in a truly ecumenical spirit. He makes a serious attempt to develop the ideas about the eucharistic sacrifice in such a way that they will be in harmony with the Reformation principle of justification by faith. He is intent on finding and eliminating those Pelagian conceptions which from ancient times have been associated with "the doctrine of the mass." In this connection it is proper to note his reluctance to accept the idea that in the Lord's Supper we offer ourselves. When all is said and done, we have nothing to offer except our insufficiency and need, unless our "offering" is included in the offering of Christ. Hebert holds that there is an inseparable connection between the pure doctrine of grace and the eucharistic sacrifice. These two must not be separated. The Reformers were inconsistent when they rejected the eucharistic sacrifice. From this point of view Hebert with his "catholic" orientation presents questions to Protestant theologians to which they must pay attention. Several of these questions we will later take up for discussion. At this point we make only a few marginal remarks on Hebert's arguments.

We must first raise the question how the eucharistic sacrifice can be Christ's own sacrifice. There is no suggestion of a repetition of the immolation on Golgotha. Hebert very decidedly rejects this idea, and he emphasizes likewise that what happens in the Lord's Supper cannot have as its purpose reconciling God by a new offering. Certain expressions, such as holding up before God the sacrifice of Christ, may indeed give the impression that God is yet unreconciled. But it would be entirely unfair to interpret Hebert's words in that sense. When the eucharist is interpreted as Christ's presentation of his own sacrifice, the reference is always to the sacrifice which the heavenly High Priest continually presents at the heavenly altar. The eucharist is placed in immediate association with this continuous act of offering. Because Christ's sacrifice has never ceased, it is continually present anew in the eucharist. In reality Christ himself is the celebrant, and therefore he is the one who brings the sacrifice before God. The argument has its basis particularly in the description of the heavenly worship in the Letter to the Hebrews.

When we listen to this presentation of Christ's sacrifice, the question inevitably arises: what is the relationship between this continuous, heavenly sacrifice of Christ, which also includes his offering in the Lord's Supper, and that sacrifice which was fulfilled once for all in his death? No matter how correct it may be according to the Scriptures that the sacrifice of Christ cannot be limited to his death, nevertheless Scripture also testifies that his act of sacrifice was completed in his death. In the light of this fact we must ask ourselves whether the offering of the heavenly High Priest lies on the same plane and is of the same kind as Christ's atoning action on earth. Or may it be that the word offering has a different meaning in these two instances? Hebert has not proposed these questions. We will not discuss them further at this point, but we will have occasion to return to them later.

Hebert interprets the eucharistic sacrifice as Christ's own sacrifice, but he also conceives of it as our offering of Christ or of his sacrifice. We must now try to clarify what might be the meaning of such a statement. We may note first that Hebert is more careful in his choice of words than Hicks, with whom he otherwise has much in common. Only once does he say that in the Lord's Supper there is "an offering of Christ," but the word "offering" stands within quotation marks, and Hebert hastens to correct the expression. He explains that it is a question of "presenting before God," "pleading" or "offering" before him, "the one sacrifice of Christ." The eucharistic sacrifice as our offering does not therefore, according to Hebert, involve an offering of Christ. We do not offer Christ, but we offer his sacrifice, bring it, plead it, include ourselves in it, participate in it. "We offer his sacrifice as participants in his sacrifice at the heavenly altar."

On what positive grounds, then, does Hebert base his claim that our eucharistic offering consists in our offering of the sacrifice of Christ? In order to answer that question we refer to the passage in which he "in a simple way" interprets the significance of our eucharistic offering. In that passage he speaks, as we have seen, about prayer as intercession. I do not expect that God will receive this my intercessory prayer on the basis of its quality, even if it were considerably better than it really is; but I "offer" it in the Lord's Supper as I bring the sacrifice of Christ and his mighty intercession before God. The question is whether this interpretation really is sufficient reason for the assertion that in the Lord's Supper we offer the sacrifice of Christ. What Hebert really says is that we bring our intercession as an offering of prayer. We know that it is weak. But we include it in the atoning act of Christ's love and in his high priestly intercession. Thus we appear before God who himself meets us in the sacrificial act of Christ's love. All this is in reality nothing else than a vivid and concrete interpretation of the meaning of prayer "in the name of Jesus." What happens is that we take refuge in, hold fast to, include ourselves, and participate in the sacrifice of Christ.

But having said all this there is really no positive reason for the assertion that we offer the sacrifice of Christ, and much less for the statement that we offer Christ. There are reasons for saying that the sacrifice of Christ is present in the eucharist, but none for saying that *we* offer this sacrifice. There are reasons for the first statement, because Christ is present as celebrant in the Lord's Supper and therefore also brings his sacrifice into the present. When Hebert interprets our eucharistic sacrifice by describing it as the inclusion of our intercession in the sacrifice and intercession of Christ, he really presents a simple and easily comprehended interpretation. The contradictions which he speaks about later are caused by his insistence that the sacrifice of Christ must be regarded as an offering which we bring, or as our sacrifice. There are no positive reasons for such an identification. In Hebert's argumentation there is a subtle transition from the one to the other. We need hardly ask for the cause of this intensive interest in making the Lord's Supper, if not our sacrifice of Christ, at least an offering of the sacrifice of Christ. The explanation is naturally that the prevalence of these terms within the "catholic" tradition exercises a very definite influence. In reality no man has ever "offered" the sacrifice of Christ. Christ's sacrifice is and remains his own act. No one except Christ himself can bring this sacrifice—none but God who sent his Son to atone for the sins of the world.

Other questions suggested by Hebert's article will be discussed in a larger context.

Some Additional Anglican Documents

We now turn first to the monumental work by Gregory Dix, *The Shape of the Liturgy.* This extensive volume of 750 pages may to some extent be regarded as the chief document representing the modern Anglican conception of the eucharist, i.e. of the High Church, Anglo-Catholic type. More than anyone else Dix has given the historical background of such an interpretation. As the title indicates, his chief concern is to present the origin and development of the eucharistic liturgy especially during the first centuries, and he does this with great learning. But his presentation of this history of the liturgy is interwoven with theological points of view and becomes therefore even more important. We cannot here undertake any extensive review of this work. We limit ourselves to two problems: the interpretation of the eucharist as an act of sacrifice, and his view of the late Middle Ages and the Reformation.

Dix develops his conception of the idea of sacrifice in a chapter entitled "The Meaning of the Eucharist." [4] He begins by emphasizing that the eucharist is an act: "Do this." It is a sacrificial act in which "something" is offered to and received by God: adoration, thanksgiving, prayer and propitiation. When the Anglican catechism says that the eucharist was ordained for "the continual remembrance of the sacrifice of the death of Christ and the benefits we receive thereby," this formula, according to Dix, betrays the narrow, "Western" conception of the sacrifice of Christ. Many, perhaps most, primitive writers would have been unwilling to accept this view of the sacrament. "It is true that the interpretation of Christ's death in particular as atoning and sacrificial was what in historical fact did more than anything else to reveal to the most primitive church the whole Messianic significance of our Lord's Person and office." But as early as apostolic times the sacrifice of Christ was seen in a larger perspective, embracing the incarnation and the eternal continuance of the sacrifice in heaven. Even though his death continued to some extent to dominate the

---

[4] Gregory Dix, *The Shape of the Liturgy* (London: Dacre Pr., 1945), p. 238ff.

interpretation of the eucharist by theologians in the early church, the wider interpretation of his sacrifice is found in the ancient liturgies.

Dix manifests a prominent tendency to use the ancient conception of the eucharist in order to examine critically the various later views of the sacrament. In the ancient church the anamnesis is related to the sacrifice of Christ as a whole. Dix points out that even in the words of institution we read: "do this in remembrance of *me,*" not in remembrance of my death. Anamnesis in the ancient church was a recalling before God of the one sacrifice of Christ in all its accomplished and effectual fulness. It is not, as in the later Middle Ages, a new sacrifice, but a perpetual recalling and energizing in the church of the one sacrifice. Dix quotes Chrysostom: "We do not offer a different sacrifice like the High Priest of old, but we ever offer the same. Or rather we offer the *anamnesis* of the sacrifice." It is the indissoluble unity of the eucharist with the sacrifice of Christ which, according to Dix, is the basis of the ancient eucharistic theology. But although the ancient writers speak in this way, the metaphysical questions about the correlation of bread and wine with body and blood simply did not exist for them. As an explanation of their naive "realism" Dix points out two factors. The sacrifice which is "re-called" is not regarded as "absent," but rather as something presently operative. Such words as "re-calling" and "re-presenting" do not convey this meaning without a special interpretation, and still less do such words as "memorial" and "remembrance." But the chief reason for the freedom of the ancient church from these metaphysical questions was the universal concentration of pre-Nicene ideas about the eucharist upon the whole rite of the eucharist as a single action. Dix emphasizes the difference between pre-Nicene and later western interpretations. They approach the question from opposite points of view. In much modern Anglican teaching there is an exact reversal of the whole primitive approach to the question. The

Anglicans start with the fact that bread and wine through the consecration "in some way" become the body and blood of Christ, and draw the conclusion that what the church does must therefore "in some sense" be the same as that which Christ did, i.e., a sacrifice. But the primitive church approached the matter from the opposite direction. The primary concern was not the sacrament but the sacrifice. Because the eucharist is primarily an act, and because the church in doing this act fulfils the will of Christ, the eucharistic act becomes of necessity his action of sacrifice, and what is offered must then be what he himself offered.

The unity (rather than union) of the church's eucharist with the sacrifice of Christ is one consequence of the general pre-Nicene insistence on the unity of Christ with the church, of the Head with the members, in one indivisible organism. This unity between Christ and the church puts its stamp on the eucharistic action as a whole and becomes intensified in the communion. The variety of interpretations of the single eucharistic action in the ancient church merge into a single conception, "whose key-thought is that the 'action' of the earthly church in the eucharist only manifests within time the eternal act of Christ as the heavenly High Priest at the altar before the throne of God, perpetually pleading His accomplished and effectual sacrifice." [5] The biblical support for this doctrine of the Lord's Supper is derived not only from the Letter to the Hebrews, but also from Ephesians and First John: "We have an advocate with the Father, Jesus Christ." Dix asserts as a fact that with two exceptions all pre-Nicene writers in the East and in the West who have developed a more elaborate doctrine of the Lord's Supper regard the sacrifice and the consecration in the eucharist as an act performed by the Lord himself. In and through his body, the church, Christ offers his flesh for the life of the world. "The eucharist is the perpetuation in time by way of *anamnesis* of His eternally accepted and complete redeeming act."

[5] *Ibid.*, p. 251.

Thus the eucharist becomes for "the catholic tradition," as for Paul, the representative act of the whole Christian life, that in which this life finds its continuance and its supreme manifestation. This manifestation implies then also that the church offers itself, that it enters into the sacrifice of Christ himself in death.

This interpretation of the eucharist which we have now reviewed is closely connected with Dix's presentation of the eschatological element in the sacrament. "In the primitive conception there is but *one eschaton,* one 'coming,' the 'coming *to* the Father' of redeemed mankind, which is the realization of the Kingdom of God. That Kingdom is realized in its fulness in the sacrifice of Christ and its acceptance—'His death and resurrection'—of which the eucharist is the *anamnesis.* 'In Him' all the redeemed enter into that Kingdom. That is the purpose and meaning of all history, however long it may continue. The eucharist is the contact of time with the eternal fact of the Kingdom of God through Jesus. In it the church in time continually, as it were, enters into its own eternal being in that Kingdom, 'in Him,' as Body of Christ, *through His act.*" [6]   One consequence of this interpretation of the eschatological element, says Dix, should be the gift to the church of that "Spirit" by which the church maintains itself in time as the body of Christ. He refers to a number of ancient documents in which the gift of the Spirit is connected with the eucharist. Through this gift the church can become what it really is. This, says Dix, is the paradox which lies at the root of all primitive eschatology: that the Christian life in this world must strive "to become what it is." "It is by the sacraments that you receive 'what you are,' your true Christian being; it is by your life that you must 'become' what they convey. . . . As S. Thomas said, the 'spiritual benefit' (*res*) received in this sacrament 'is the unity of the mystical body'—and in the New Testament this unity is above all 'the unity of the

* *Ibid.,* p. 265.

Spirit.' " [7] In this quotation Dix makes Thomas represent the central conception of the Lord's Supper found in the New Testament and in the ancient church.

This conception, however, was supplanted in the late Middle Ages, whose theology and practice Dix sharply criticizes. Theology busied itself with all kinds of subtleties in the interpretation of the doctrine of transubstantiation, with the result that piety went its own way in a definitely individualistic direction. Communion by the laity became rare. The emphasis was laid more and more on the individual adoration of the host. The book, *Imitatio Christi*, is concerned exclusively with the individual soul's devotion in the presence of the sacrament; there is hardly a single mention of the eucharist "as the life and unity of the church." This individualistic orientation, remains, according to Dix, both in the Reformation and the Counter-Reformation.

The background of the sixteenth-century conflict about the Lord's Supper, according to Dix, was not the New Testament, from which each side quoted isolated passages, and much less the ancient church, of which neither side knew very much. It was rather the rite as then practiced in the late Medieval church. Dix summarizes his criticism in the following points.[8] 1) The notion of the eucharist as a corporate action had been transformed. The significance of the eucharist as an action of the whole church had largely disappeared. Especially at the manifold private masses the priest functioned alone. He brought the offering. Normally the celebrant alone communed. 2) Although the masses depended on the sacrifice on Golgotha, each individual sacerdotal offering had a separate efficacy and value of its own. "Thus ten masses were necessarily and determinably worth more than five." 3) The use of Latin reduced the function of hearing the mass to small usefulness for the laity. The liturgy became something foreign, and the

---

[7] *Ibid.*, p. 267.
[8] *Ibid.*, p. 615ff.

brief prayers given to the laity to read while mass was being said were of little value. 4) Participation by the congregation became concentrated on the one moment in the rite, the elevation, especially introduced in the eleventh century in order that they might see; and seeing they adored. 5) The most momentous distinction of all between Medieval western and primitive, eucharistic thought was the almost total loss of the eschatological conception. Dix points out that the prayers used in the Lord's Supper were concerned almost exclusively with the death on the cross. The total effect was to emphasize the reference to the past in Paul's words that in the eucharist "you proclaim the Lord's death," to the neglect of the eschatological implications of what follows, "till he come." This restriction of the act of salvation to Golgotha created serious difficulties. When the reference is confined to an act in the past, two possibilities are open: either the Lord's Supper is purely a mental remembrance, or else in some way a repetition and renewal of the sacrifice of Christ. According to Dix the Reformers —and here they are taken en masse, although Cranmer is especially mentioned—held to the first alternative; the later Middle Ages had adopted the second.

According to the Reformers there is, therefore, no real sacrifice in the eucharist. "The external rite is at the most an acted memorial, *reminding* us of something no longer present." Bread and wine are only "signs." The eucharistic action, if we may speak of it as such, is an action concerned with the individual soul. It has lost its corporate significance. The reason for this development was that the Reformers not only still further emphasized the relationship of the Lord's Supper to the passion, but did so without taking into account "its eternal consequences."

It is unnecessary to review further the exposition of the Reformation which Dix here presents. He admits without reservation that the Reformation was necessary because of the grave mistakes made in the later Middle Ages, but he finds its weakness in the fact that it was negatively dependent on the opposition. We may add just a few words about his treatment of Luther, which does not betray any deeply penetrating insight. On the basis of the Bible, says Dix, Luther maintained the real presence, but he rejected sacrifice in any other sense than as an offering of prayer. The body and blood of Christ is not offered to God, but to the people, to the communicants. "There is still a eucharistic action, even an action of Christ in the eucharist—but the church does not enter into it. Her part is only to prepare herself for it and *receive it*. We can see here the effect of Luther's perpetual primary assumption about the end of religion, that it is not the worship of God but the comfort of man." [9] In what follows Dix even asserts that for Luther faith is always not faith in Christ as Redeemer, but faith in my redemption by him. He characterizes Luther's conception of salvation as "self-regarding and self-generated." He closes his chapter on the Reformation with the statement: "I believe that the history of protestantism itself indicates that they [the Protestants] were the chief and most permanent sufferers by the accumulated mistakes of the mediaeval Latin church." [10]

One of the most important, and presumably the most influential, of the writings which deal with the problem we are discussing is the book by A. M. Ramsey, *The Gospel and the Catholic Church.* Although this book is not a direct contribution to the ecumenical debate, it nevertheless is ecumenically oriented. Ramsey is convinced that Anglicanism has certain special qualifications enabling it to uphold a common Christian perspective in relation to both "Latin" and "Protestant" prejudices. When he seeks to demonstrate these Anglican possibilities, he is concerned first of all with maintaining an "organic" view of the church over against legalism and individualism, then also with showing how ministry, episcopacy,

[9] *Ibid.,* p. 635.
[10] *Ibid.,* p. 639.

and apostolic succession are connected with the gospel and receive their significance "on account of their evangelical content." We cannot discuss these problems here, but must confine ourselves to his presentation of the idea of sacrifice in the Lord's Supper and his attitude toward the Reformation.

Ramsey, like the other Anglican authors we have quoted, conceives of Christ's act of sacrifice from a twofold point of view: the eternal sacrifice, and the sacrifice in time. But his view is unique in this respect: the "eternal" sacrifice not only involves a continuation of the earthly sacrifice, but also expresses an eternal intertrinitarian relationship, reflecting the eternal attitude of the Son to the Father. This is Ramsey's interpretation of the words in the Letter to the Hebrews: "A priest forever according to the order of Melchizedek." The Son forever possesses the character of one who gives his life utterly in love. Ramsey points also to the word in the Gospel of John about the eternal love of the Son to the Father, and the Father to the Son. This eternal priesthood of Christ is revealed in time and in history through the life and death of the incarnate Son. The essence of the sacrifice is the giving of life, "the life whereof the abiding characteristic is to have died. Thus priest eternally and priest on earth, our Lord is priest *now* in His relation to the Father, forever giving to the Father as Son of Man a life of which the death once died in history is the revealing mark and character. . . . The Christians look back to the sacrifice of Calvary and they look up to the eternal sacrifice which it reveals." [11] But this is not something which happens merely "outside" the Christians but also "within" them. The body of Christ, the church, shares in his priesthood, for in his body he lives and gives his life in the midst of pain and sin. Hence Peter describes the Christians as "a royal priesthood." Since Christ through his eternal nature and through his act in history is a High Priest, and

[11] Arthur M. Ramsey, *The Gospel and the Catholic Church* (New York: Longmans, 1936), p. 114f.

since his body shares in his priesthood, "it follows also that the Eucharist, wherein the whole truth of Christ and His Church is focused, is an act of sacrifice."

The conception of sacrifice is therefore inseparably connected with the eucharist. The sacrificial language became richer. Cyprian is the first one who speaks of the sacrifice in the eucharist as an offering of the body and blood of Christ: "his passion is the offering which we make." Ramsey maintains that Cyprian here simply expresses that which is inherent in the eucharist, since it is inherent in Christ himself. Behind this language there is the gospel, since Christ's act in history is the source of what Christians do. And behind this conception of the sacrifice there is also the doctrine of the church as the body.

Misinterpretations arise when this twofold background is ignored. Ramsey mentions three such misinterpretations. One of them arises when the sacrifice is identified exclusively with the death of Christ on the cross. The result of this was the Medieval conception of the mass as a repetition of the sacrifice on Golgotha and the reaction of the Reformation against the idea of sacrifice in general. Another misconception derives from the separation of the action of Christ from the Father, forgetting that the initiative to the reconciliation is taken by the Father, and that the sacrifice is the action of God in Christ and in his body, the church. A third mis-interpretation of the sacrifice arises because of a false separation between the ministerial office and the church. This leads to the conception that the priest as an individual and in virtue of rights inherent in himself offers in the mass a separate sacrifice to God, rather than acting on behalf of the Lord and his whole church.[12]

With this as a background Ramsey presents his evaluation of Luther. Luther's revolt "was a revival of the gospel of God, and also a revival of many vital elements in the doctrine of the one body which springs from the gospel. It meant the recovery of truths

[12] *Ibid.,* pp. 113-118.

about the church which are central in the teaching of Paul and Augustine and in the inner meaning of Catholicism. The revolt was soon perverted by negative and individualistic conceptions; but meanwhile the official church had lost its chance. It met the revolt with the voice of authority, it failed to see the inner meaning of Luther's demands, and it set about to reform itself along lines of efficiency and deep spirituality, yet with the crisis of the gospel still unfaced." In spite of all piety and heroism the Counter-Reformation did not regain the inner meaning of the word "catholic." [13]

Ramsey summarizes his conception of Luther in the following appraisal. Luther reintroduced not only the Pauline doctrine of justification but also the Pauline teaching about the body of Christ. But Lutheranism drifted into individualism because of a false opposition between the inward and the outward. Luther was unable to see the significance which church order had for apostolic Christianity, and therefore missed an important element in Paul, in the New Testament, and in the gospel.[14] In regard to the doctrine of the Lord's Supper Ramsey says that Luther's doctrine of the ubiquity of Christ's risen body involved him in crudities and difficulties, but that the Luther who wrote on the table at the Marburg Conference *hoc est corpus meum* belongs to the history of positive sacramentalism.

Before we leave the Anglican documents it might be proper to note a book by E. L. Mascall published in 1953 under the title *Corpus Christi*. What makes this book particularly significant from our point of view is that the author analyzes and evaluates some of the Roman theologians who in recent years have studied "the significance of the eucharistic sacrifice" from fresh points of view. This confrontation throws light also on the relationship between modern Anglican and Roman theologians.

[13] *Ibid.*, p. 171.
[14] *Ibid.*, p. 190ff.

Mascall finds that lately much has happened in Roman theology which might enable us to move out of the deadlock which has characterized the relationship between Roman and Protestant theologians during four centuries; a deadlock which has been caused primarily by the theory of the mass as a repetition of the sacrifice on Golgotha. After he has dealt with the book, *Mysterium fidei,* by Maurice de la Taille (1915), which in many respects was a pioneering work, Mascall emphasizes especially the work of the Roman theologians Vonier and Masure.

Abbot Anscar Vonier published in 1925 the work entitled *A Key to the Doctrine of the Eucharist.* For Vonier the fundamental fact about the eucharist is that it is a sacrament; and the fundamental fact about a sacrament is that it is a sign, but a sign of a very special kind. Its purpose is to re-present, to make present, to effect, that which is represented. The sacrament is a sign which has effective causality, a sign which brings about that which it signifies. This means that the eucharistic presence of Christ is entirely real, but it is of an entirely different type from his presence on earth before his ascension and his presence in heaven after it.

The eucharistic presence exists because and only because Christ by his institution and promise has attached it to certain visible signs. Mascall thinks that Vonier, in the medieval manner, is inclined to identify sacrifice too exclusively with death, but this is an emphasis which can easily be corrected without detriment to his special contribution. What is of primary importance is his realization that the sacrificial character of the mass is not an event that happens to Christ after his ascension, and which should in some sense repeat or imitate his death. What happens is rather that the whole sacrificial action of Christ becomes sacramentally present in his church. It is not a matter of repeating or complementing his sacrifice; it is simply the sacrifice itself which is present, and it is present only because the sacramental elements are the divinely ordained effective signs of it. The inner reality which the sacramental

signs contain, the whole redemptive act of Christ, is simply sacramentally present. If we ask what Christ is doing now, the answer is that he is reigning in glory and interceding for us before
the Father's throne. The mass is a sacrifice, not because Christ
dies on our altars, but because bread and wine are divinely ordained signs of the presence of the sacrifice. The one sacrifice is
present in the church as "the ground of the church's existence and
the source of its life." [15]

Mascall finds the same fundamental view of the sacrament in
the writings of Eugène Masure (*Le Sacrifice du Chef* [1932], English translation, *The Christian Sacrifice* [1940]; *Le Sacrifice du
Corps Mystique* [1950]). The sacrifice is an effective symbol. As
a sign instituted by Christ the sacrament is rich enough to include
the reality of that which it symbolizes. The sacrament is "a sign
possessing, in virtue of its author, the value which it signifies." The
terms symbol and sign do not then have the impoverished and
pitiable significance they have in Protestantism. With this view
of the sacrament Masure combines a determined criticism of that
Roman, post-Reformation theology which in one form or another
regarded the mass as a repetition of the sacrifice on Golgotha. The
support for his own conception of the eucharist he finds in Thomas
and the Council of Trent, and consequently claims that he is following the authentic, catholic tradition. Parenthetically Mascall
observes that the doctrine of the sacrifice of the mass which he
criticizes does not belong only to post-Reformation times but can
be found also in the Middle Ages.[16]

As we have seen, it is the intention of Mascall to discover tendencies in modern Roman theology which may serve to bring the
Roman-Protestant discussion out of the long "deadlock." In this
study he pays special attention to the candid criticism which Roman theologians direct against the theory of the eucharist as a

[15] Eric L. Mascall, *Corpus Christi, Essays on the Church and the Eucharist*
(New York: Longmans, 1953), p. 94ff.
[16] *Ibid.*, p. 98ff.

repetition of the sacrifice on Golgotha, and also to the deeper understanding of the nature of the sacramental "sign." The essential point, according to Mascall, is that in the sacrament the whole life of Christ from the incarnation to the ascension is conceived of as an offering to the Father and is present "not as a new event in history, but as a permanent reality communicated to the church under the sacramental signs." It might be objected, he says, that this emphasis on sacramental significance is typical of the western church, and that the word *Mysterion,* the chief designation of the eucharist in the Eastern Orthodox church, contains no particular suggestion of a sign. According to Mascall, this difference may indicate that sacramental theology has been more fully developed in the West. But there is no real contradiction. "The elements are signs—effectual signs—in virtue of Christ's institution and promise, not in virtue of their physical properties. It is only by faith that they are recognized as being signs at all. The sign is a sign of a mystery; and the mystery is a mystery of a sign." [17]

[17] *Ibid.,* p. 107ff.

4

Two Roman Voices

Before we close this review of contemporary ecumenical discussions about the eucharist with some questions, we should say a few words about modern Roman theories of the Supper. In reality this, too, belongs in the ecumenical debate. Although the Roman theologians cannot officially participate in ecumenical deliberations, the ecumenical movement is not unconcerned about or indifferent to ideas that emanate from Rome, nor are Roman theologians indifferent to what happens elsewhere in Christendom. Mascall's work is not the only indication that the reorientation which undoubtedly is taking place within Roman theology raises new hope in ecumenical circles. We have noted that Hebert, for instance, gives expression to such expectations. There are many indications, too, that not only Anglicans but also Lutheran and Reformed theologians follow the development within Roman theology with great interest. We cannot present here an extensive review of Roman theology of the sacrament. We must confine ourselves to two characteristic documents. There are good reasons for us to return to the work of Masure which Mascall reviewed. There are many points of view in this work which Mascall has not touched upon, but which must be considered in order to prevent the picture from becoming too one-sided. There are two questions which especially claim our attention.

One question concerns the presence of Christ in the Supper. It is true that Masure strongly emphasizes the character of the

51

sacrament as "an effective symbol," a symbol which contains the reality and "effects what it represents." It is also true that from this point of view Masure severely criticizes the post-Tridentine theories which in one way or another speak of the sacrifice in the eucharist as a repetition of the sacrifice on Golgotha, either as a figurative, representative immolation, or a real and renewed immolation. But what must be noted here is that Masure combines this symbolic realism with the doctrine of transubstantiation. "In the Sacrifice of the Mass the Church takes bread and wine and first seems to use them as the sign or symbol of her adoration. But . . . however pure and beautiful these oblations may be, they have no power to please God. But when God changes them into the Body and Blood of the sole Victim acceptable to Him, then, by an inconceivably triumphant transformation, our Sacrifice receives the perfect proof of the divine appeasement. For the Church, by means of this transubstantiation, is put in possession of the one efficacious victim, as the victim of *her* Sacrifice, and with this of all the religious achievement which she sought: the church shares in an upward movement that perfect adoration of which the Sacred Humanity of Christ is the temple; downwards she sees coming to her through the accepted Victim all divine favours, all the Father's good pleasure." [1] Masure emphasizes that transubstantiation is the reason why all this can happen in the sacrament.

What Masure says here sheds light also on the other question concerning the sacrifice of the church. In the preface to the English edition the translator, a Roman theologian, asks how often sermons on the mass are preached which really tell *why* the sacrifice is offered and what it is all about. He adds that he believes Masure has provided the answers to these questions. But it is not so easy to discover his reasons "why we sacrifice" and what the sacrifice involves. We might ask first of all whether what is offered

[1] Eugène Masure, *The Christian Sacrifice*, tr. by Dom Illtyd Trethowan (New York: Kenedy, 1944), p. 14ff.

is the sacrifice of Christ or Christ himself. The first alternative seems to be connected with "the symbolic realism," the second with the emphasis on the doctrine of transubstantiation. Why must the church offer this sacrifice? We may note the following statement as an answer: If in the Lord's Supper it were only a question of a communion with the victim, something would be lacking, "at least psychologically." "Human nature seems to demand more, and the rights of God seem to claim from us more efforts, greater adoration." [2] The question why we, the church, must sacrifice seems to be given a twofold answer. We are to offer Christ, or his sacrifice, because by so doing our adoration becomes perfect, and because through the divine act of transubstantiation we receive a perfect proof of the divine reconciliation. Consequently the emphasis is not really on our sacrifice as such; it is the divine transformation which furnishes the confident proof of the reality of the atonement. Masure justifies the right of the church to offer this eucharistic sacrifice with these words: When the Lord at the institution of the eucharist gave "the apostles the power and the precept to renew this action, he gave to his church at the same time the right and the duty of making Him the victim every morning on her altars." [3] But this sacrifice would be fruitless were it not through transubstantiation changed into the sacrifice of Christ. "There are therefore in the Mass, if one may dare to put it so, two sacrifices:" through the change "the Savior's sacrifice is substituted for her own, and is made one with it." [4]

One of the most important Roman interpretations of the Lord's Supper in recent times is Joseph Pascher's *Eucharistia, Gestalt und Vollzug* (first edition 1952, second revised edition 1953). The book is written as a commentary on the Roman liturgy and is characterized by clarity and breadth of perspective.

We turn first to Pascher's presentation of the sacrifice in the Lord's Supper. The Roman church teaches, says Pascher, not that

[2] *Ibid.*, p. 237.   [3] *Ibid.*, p. 241.   [4] *Ibid.*, p. 248.

Christ offers himself continually anew as if new acts of sacrifice were added to the sacrifice on the cross. It teaches rather that the one and only sacrifice is presented again (*wieder dargestellt werde*) in the symbolism of the cult. The expression *repraesentare* (*Vergegenwärtigung*) used in the Tridentinum is capable of different interpretations. Pascher maintains, however, that it is not a question of a number of acts of sacrifice beside the historical sacrifice made once for all. At the same time he points out that the word "present" involves something more than a mere likeness. It is not a question of a merely figurative presentation of the body and blood of the Lord, but rather of the reality in symbolic form. When the cultic act places his sacrifice in our midst, this act really brings with it the once-for-all sacrifice of Christ. When we here speak of a "renewal" of Christ's sacrifice on the cross, the meaning is not that what happened on the cross now is performed for the second or third time, but that the once-for-all sacrifice is made present again (*vergegenwärtigt wird*).[5] We may also remark that, although Pascher speaks here about the sacrifice of Christ on the cross, he does not imply that his sacrifice was restricted to his death on the cross. The resurrection and the ascension also belong to his sacrifice. "Through his resurrection and ascension he has entered the Holy of Holies and completes there eternally the offering of his body and blood." This is involved in anamnesis, and the church therefore prays in its liturgy that God may send his angels to carry the sacrifice in the Lord's Supper into the presence of the Father in the Holy of Holies.[6]

One characteristic feature of Pascher's presentation is his strong emphasis on the idea of fellowship in the Lord's Supper. This appears both in his analysis of the participation of the faithful in the sacrifice and in his insistence on the central significance of communion.

[5] Joseph Pascher, *Eucharistia, Gestalt und Vollzug* (1953), p. 24ff.
[6] *Ibid.*, p. 150ff.

Do the believers participate in the eucharistic act of sacrifice? It is clear, says Pascher, that the consecrated priest himself "performs the sacrificial symbolism" in behalf of Christ. But the problem is whether the believers in some sense co-operate in or only behold the sacrifice. This problem has become highly relevant due to the liturgical movement within the church. Various texts in the liturgy indicate a co-operation in the sacrifice. But theological pronouncements have frequently rejected this idea, and in doing so have appealed to the decisions of the Council of Trent, whose statements in opposition to the Reformation were intended to maintain the reality of the eucharistic sacrifice through the office of the consecrated priest. The Roman catechism, to be sure, distinguishes between an external and an inner priesthood. It states that in virtue of their inner priesthood the faithful are to bring forth spiritual oblations. Such a spiritual, sacrificial service is of great religions significance, according to Pascher, but it has the character of sacrifice only "in an improper sense." The question remains whether "the priesthood of the baptized participates in the real act of sacrifice, or if their offering consists only in prayers, hymns and oblations." Pascher answers this question of the participation of the faithful in the "real" sacrifice in the affirmative, and he supports his answer by a reference to the communion and "connection" of the faithful with the consecrated priest. He appeals to statements of Pius XII in the encyclical *Mediator Dei,* where the Pope asserts that the faithful "bring the sacrifice not merely through the hands of the priest but also in a certain sense (*quodammodo*) together with him." Co-operation in the sacrifice becomes a reality through the congregation's "connection" with the consecrated, officiating priest. The eucharist appears from this point of view as a sacrificial fellowship. The visible signs of this sacrificial fellowship are not to be found in the act of sacrifice itself, because this is performed by the priest alone. The sign is to be found rather in "the hierarchical structure of the table fellowship. Here the participation in the sacrifice becomes a sacramental reality. If this is so, the table fellowship becomes of tremendous importance in the eucharistic sacrifice." [7]

It is obvious that from this point of view Pascher must lay great emphasis on communion. But there are also other reasons for this emphasis: the fact that the Lord's Supper creates fellowship, and the liturgical movement's striving for lay participation in the mass. But no matter how strongly the communion is emphasized, the communion of the congregation is not absolutely essential. The mass does not depend on the communion, but it is "more complete" when this takes place. Even for these two statements Pascher can refer to the encyclical *Mediator Dei*.[8]

These Roman documents under discussion, as well as many others, strive to define the relationship between the sacrifice of Christ once for all and the eucharistic sacrifice in such a way that the latter implies a re-presentation, a *Vergegenwärtigung*, a recalling of the former. The intention is to define the sacrifice of the mass in such a way that it does not detract from the one sacrifice of Christ. The eucharistic sacrifice must not be understood as a kind of complement to the once-for-all sacrifice, nor as an independent sacrifice beside the other. This argument follows "the Thomas-Augustinian line" in Roman theology but with severe criticism of post-Tridentine theories. There is no doubt but that this criticism strikes also at conceptions which were prevalent during the Middle Ages and the Reformation. It is significant that many are very critical of the defense against Luther's attack which was presented during the Reformation. One example of this is E. Iserloh's criticism of Eck in his *Der Kampf um die Messe in den ersten Jahren der Auseinandersetzung mit Luther* (1952).

At the same time and in accordance with ancient tradition the idea of sacrifice remains dominant in modern Roman theology of

[7] *Ibid.*, p. 270ff.
[8] *Ibid.*, p. 33.

the sacrament. The eucharistic sacrifice involves not only the doctrine that the Lord's Supper makes the sacrifice of Christ present and living, but also the theory that the Supper is to be interpreted as our sacrifice, a presentation by the church of the sacrifice of Christ through the consecrated priest. Even the idea of communion can be incorporated under this point of view, as we have seen, and be regarded as a visible sign of the sacrificial fellowship in which the faithful participate through the officiating priest. This double aspect of the eucharistic sacrifice is very prevalent. There can be no question, says Masure, of "doing again" the great and only sacrifice. The mass "does not begin the redemption over again, but it takes hold of it, possesses the sacrifice, communicating to us all its fruits. . . . The victim already exists, but *we have to make it ours.*" According to Masure these words in italics have a double meaning. "To make ours" means "to get possession of," or "to do again on our own account." [9] This double aspect of the eucharistic sacrifice is possible only through transubstantiation.

[9] Masure, *op. cit.*, p. 284.

5

Review and Questions

The most important task for the ecumenical discussion must be to grasp clearly the actual, present antitheses. It then becomes self-evident that we must consider the Reformation, since this event has caused the sharpest differences in the history of Christianity. This is especially true of the interpretation of Holy Communion, and most especially about the eucharist as an act of sacrifice. It is not surprising, therefore, that the writers of the documents we have examined generally have found it necessary, in one way or another, directly or indirectly, to define their attitude to the Reformation. What happened at that time cannot be bypassed. The questions then raised and the decisions made exercise an influence even today.

As we review what has been said about the Reformation by various writers, we find a general assumption that it is possible to note a certain change of attitude toward the original formulations. Thus the Reformed theologian Torrance says that the antitheses between Roman and Evangelical doctrines of the Lord's Supper "have become considerably narrowed," but he adds that the difference is nevertheless very deep. Representative Anglican theologians—Hicks, Hebert, Dix, and Ramsey—desire above all to emphasize the possibilities of overcoming the divisions between "Catholic" and "Protestant" which have appeared in modern times. These possibilities have arisen because modern Roman theologians have attempted to reform the doctrine of the mass, and because Protestants have found that the idea of sacrifice belongs more legitimately to the Christian tradition than the Reformers were willing to admit. These Anglican theologians maintain that Anglicanism has special qualifications to lead the discussion between Catholicism and Protestantism out of the deadlock which has characterized the situation for a long time. They believe it is possible to hold fast a "catholicity" which accepts whatever was legitimate in the criticism urged by the Reformation, but which at the same time adopts a wider outlook than Roman Catholicism, which neither in the Counter-Reformation nor in modern times has been able to overcome its truncated conception of true catholicity.

The Anglican theologians criticise the eucharistic doctrine and practice of the late Middle Ages which involved a false conception of the eucharistic sacrifice, eliminated the communion, and substituted a thoroughgoing individualism for the conception of the church underlying the ancient doctrine of the eucharist. They acknowledge the well-grounded criticism of the Medieval doctrine of the mass by the Reformers, approve their idea of the central significance of communion and their reaffirmation that the eucharist is an action of the church. But they also find that the Reformation was in various ways negatively dependent on the conception which they criticised, that the struggle against the sacrifice of the mass led to a radical rejection of the idea of sacrifice in general, and that the Reformation, too, in spite of its original intention ended up in a strict individualism. Both the appreciation and the criticism of the Reformation appear in variable forms in the different authors. Dix is the most critical, especially in his suggestion that Protestants have suffered most from the accumulated mistakes of the late Medieval church.

In view of what has been said here about the attitude to the Reformation in the various ecumenical documents, both commendation and criticism, and about the hope of transcending the traditional antitheses, it is imperative that we devote a section of this study to the Reformation. We do not, however, go to the Reformation in the expectation of finding final answers to the problems in the interpretation of Holy Communion. The Reformation has never ascribed any final authority either to the Reformers or to the confessions. The purpose is rather to examine, to the extent necessary in this connection, the doctrine of the Lord's Supper in the Reformation, and especially its attitude to the idea of sacrifice. We limit ourselves here to a consideration of the Lutheran Reformation. This limitation does not imply that other branches of the Reformation do not deserve attention. The reasons are, first, the necessity of limiting this study to a reasonable proportion, and second, the fact that in the Lutheran Reformation we meet the first, original, powerful impact of the Reformation's intentions.

When we move from the ecumenical discussion to the Reformation, there is no lack of questions. We may inquire concerning the legitimacy of the commendations and criticisms which have been directed toward it. We may also ask whether and to what extent the discussion between "catholic" and "reformed" thinking has moved away from the so-called deadlock, and whether there is any reasonable hope of overcoming the centuries-old antitheses. But all these questions may be gathered up finally in the one central question: what was the essential element in the Reformation, that which constituted the foundation of its critical as well as positive statements?

From what we have now said it is clear that we cannot stop with the Reformation. When it renounces all claims of being a final authority, it points away from itself to the Bible. A third section will therefore have to deal with the Lord's Supper in the Bible. This is necessary in order that we may discover whether the Reformers' doctrine of the Lord's Supper contains not only elements of temporary significance, but also something that is genuinely and permanently Christian.

In the ecumenical discussion we have frequently encountered, aside from commendation, the assertion that because of its polemical attitude the Reformation has lost something of the richness of the eucharistic thought of the ancient church. We cannot silently ignore such statements. It is obvious that in the ancient church there were points of view which are not to be found directly in the Bible. This does not imply that these points of view are not genuinely Christian. They may very well have developed on biblical ground and possess the biblical power of life. The decisive question is whether that which has been added harmonizes or stands in conflict with the fundamental biblical conception. When in this section we discuss the biblical points of view, we do so in conformity with demands which the ecumenical conversations have expressed more and more fully and insistently. We close this study finally with a section of fundamental and systematic character.

Part II

The Reformation

6

Ecumenicity and the Reformation

That the ecumenical discussion again and again reverts to the Reformation is not primarily due to the historical significance of this event, nor to the fact that the decisions then made are continually relevant. The reason is rather that we seem to have found new possibilities of escaping from the stereotyped formulations in which discussion about the Lord's Supper has been confined for centuries. The time has come, it is said, when more fruitful and realistic conversations about the controversial eucharistic problems may be carried on across confessional boundaries.

It is undeniable that the interconfessional polemic has for a long time been stereotyped and monotonous. It has become like trench warfare in which the belligerents attack one another from their fortified positions. But a new mobility has appeared in these ecumenical discussions—which, of course, ought not to be compared to warfare but rather to peace negotiations.

The attempts to escape from the traditional positions have been most in evidence in regard to the question of the presence of sacrifice in the eucharist, i.e., the question which was the primary cause of the struggle with Rome. In our review of the discussions we have discovered such attempts among Lutherans, Reformed, and Anglicans, and even among some Roman Catholics. Both Lutheran and Reformed theologians have sensed the need for a re-examination of the place and significance of the idea of sacrifice. They have manifested a willingness to assume a more positive attitude than was possible in the anti-Roman polemic during the Reformation. It is evident, however, that all such attempts must be fully aware of the tremendous dangers connected with this idea of sacrifice; dangers which the Reformation has pointed out very clearly. Unless this is done, the losses will be greater than the gains. Roman representatives have been anxious to maintain that the criticisms voiced by the Reformation were directed against corruptions, but did not affect what they regard as the "classical," catholic conceptions. They have sought to present a doctrine of the mass from which these corruptions have been removed. The position taken in this matter by some Anglican theologians is rather interesting. They seem to appear as a kind of referee between Rome and the Reformation. With their strongly patristic orientation they are ready to approve the essential points in the criticism and the positive contributions of the Reformation. But at the same time they maintain that the interpretation of the Lord's Supper involved some serious losses when compared with that of the Bible and the ancient church. But if the Reformers' interpretation lacked catholicity, so also does the post-Tridentine Roman theology. The Anglican theology of the sacrament claims, therefore, a higher degree of catholicity than either the Roman or the Protestant.

The problem of sacrifice has dominated the ecumenical discussion of the Lord's Supper. The other great controversial question of the Reformation, the real presence, has not received comparable attention. As we look at the ecumenical documents, we seem to detect a certain reticence in regard to this subject. It appears that no one really wants to question the actuality of "the real presence." At the same time there seems to be a consciousness that a deeper penetration of this subject would reveal some very decisive differences. This whole problem has been avoided for the present, but the ecumenical discussion will sooner or later have to take it up for a thorough investigation. This is even more imperative because, as our study of the Reformation will reveal, the problems of "the eucharistic sacrifice" and the real presence are closely related.

If we examine the evaluation of Luther and the Reformation found in the Anglican documents which we have studied, it appears that judgments have frequently been influenced by what has been found in later Protestantism. In the interest of objectivity and clarity we must make certain distinctions. We must distinguish between the ideas concerning the Lord's Supper found in Luther himself, and the elements which came to have a decisive influence in the subsequent development. We must also determine how far later factors, such as Pietism and the Enlightenment, have exercised a transforming influence.

If we now turn to the stabilized conceptions and confessional antitheses which characterize seventeenth-century orthodoxy, the Lutheran doctrine of the Lord's Supper may be expressed in two chief points: (1) The Lord's Supper is not a *sacrificium* but a sacramental means of grace through which the gift of forgiveness of sins is bestowed; and (2) The presence of the body and blood of Christ is asserted in the doctrine of consubstantiation. The first point is directed against the Roman doctrine of the mass; the second partly against those who deny the real presence of the body and blood of Christ and partly the Roman doctrine of transubstantiation. The first statement expresses a genuine Lutheran concern, but that is hardly true of the second. Consubstantiation was not one of Luther's characteristic terms, and it does not express his intention. In reality Luther very seldom used this term. "Consubstantiation" and "transubstantiation" are both scholastic terms derived from Nominalism, and the line of thought developed by this post-Reformation theology is thoroughly scholastic. We cannot deny, of course, that Luther, too, indulges at times in scholastic reasonings, but his real interest goes entirely contrary to all scholasticism.

A review of Luther's own writings on the subject of the Lord's

Supper discloses a rich variety of ideas which have only partly found expression within confessional Lutheranism. This is true especially of the celebrated writing of 1519: "A Treatise Concerning the Blessed Sacrament of the Holy and True Body of Christ" (See chap. 7, n. 2). It would be difficult to find in all Christendom anything comparable to the rich variety of ideas contained within this relatively small treatise of a few pages.

There are several reasons why some of Luther's ideas about the Lord's Supper have been relatively neglected within the church of the Reformation. Two of these are especially important: the polemical situation, and the fact that the two writings which exercised the greatest influence on instruction and the worship life —the Catechisms and Luther's two liturgical formularies—were written during the period (1520) when the strife about the doctrine of the Lord's Supper was at its most crucial point. The Lutheran doctrine of the Lord's Supper was developed in conflict with misinterpretations which had to be rejected. One result of this fact was that the fundamental conception of the Lord's Supper became more clearly and definitely expressed than it had been in Luther's earlier writings about the sacrament. But at the same time it meant that a great many points of view were neglected because they had no direct bearing on the controversy.

7

Treatise on the Blessed Sacrament
and the Small Catechism

In the *Treatise on the Blessed Sacrament* (1519), Luther had not yet developed his doctrine of the Lord's Supper with the decisiveness which characterizes his later writings. Although the principles of the Reformation were by this time clearly worked out, Luther continued to accept both theories and practices which he later rejected. He did not object to the practice of giving only the bread to the laity, and he talked about a "change" of the elements, even though this term has no specific doctrinal significance. He manifests a critical attitude toward the celebration of the sacrifice of the mass, but his criticism has a different frame of reference from what occurs later when the conflict about the Lord's Supper became more intense.

It is, however, proper to begin our analysis of the Reformation with a study of this treatise. There are two reasons for this: First, because in this little pamphlet one of the fundamental principles of the Reformation finds clear and vigorous expression; and second, because this writing contains a number of elements which have become obscured and relatively ignored in the later polemical writings about the Lord's Supper.

"The Treatise Concerning the Blessed Sacrament of the Holy and True Body of Christ" is a great paean of praise, a prose hymn celebrating the glory of the eucharist. There can be no question

about what is the central point in the treatise. All agree that the
center of it all is communion. Communion in the Lord's Supper
involves an incorporation with Christ and his saints. "The *mystery*
of sacramental fellowship," says Brilioth, "has indeed rarely found
nobler expression than in this little writing. The rediscovery of
the idea of communion is the greatest positive contribution of the
Reformation in regard to the eucharist; it is of more value than
all the criticisms of the mass." Luther has here "rediscovered the
Pauline mystery of sacramental fellowship." [1]

The Lord's Supper means, therefore, a participation in Christ and
communio sanctorum, "to be received into the community of
saints, and to be incorporated into Christ's spiritual body and
made a member of Him. . . . To receive the bread and wine of this
sacrament, then, is nothing else than to receive a sure sign of this
fellowship and incorporation with Christ and all saints." [2] In this
connection Luther refers to I Corinthians 10:17. This communion
theme recurs again and again in this treatise.

What is most remarkable is the vigorous and living view of the
church which undergirds Luther's interpretation of the Lord's
Supper. Holy Communion is not something which the individual
guest enjoys in isolation. The essential point is that he is brought
into communion "with Christ and all the saints," and therefore
with that church which is "the spiritual body of Christ" (*Christi
corpus mysticum*). Luther loves to use the formula "Christ and
all saints." The meaning is not that Christ and the saints are somehow equal. His idea is very clearly biblical. Christ and his church
are inseparable. Where Christ is there are also "his saints." To
have fellowship in *communio sanctorum* is primarily to be united
with Christ, for the church is "His spiritual body."

We must also note that when Luther says that the bread and
wine of the sacrament are "a sure sign of this fellowship and

[1] Brilioth, *op. cit.,* p. 97.
[2] Martin Luther, *Works of Martin Luther,* Weimar Ausgabe (cited hereafter
as *WA*), 2, 743. In the Philadelphia Edition (cited hereafter as *PE*), II, 10.

incorporation with Christ," as he does in several passages of this treatise, the meaning is not that the sign is of merely symbolical nature. The "sign" of which he speaks is not simply the bread and the wine; it also includes the eating and drinking and the whole eucharistic act. The Lord's Supper is a meal of fellowship, and in its "divine sign" includes the reality of fellowship. Fellowship with Christ and his saints is here "pledged, granted, and imparted." [3]

What is the significance of this communion and what gift does it bestow? Luther answers that it is a twofold help: against sin and against death. The perspective is both present and eschatological. The help against sin appears from two points of view, although both are closely related. From one point of view communion means that we are not alone in our struggle against sin. Christ and his saints fight with us, and this gives us comfort and strength. But the help is not confined to such a participation in the struggle. It is not only a question of "with us" but "for us" and "instead of us." This is the basis of God's forgiveness, of the fact that he does not reckon sin "according to his strict judgment." When Luther in this connection uses the formula "Christ and his saints," it is obvious that the emphasis is on Christ and his work. In this sacrament, says Luther, the immeasurable grace and mercy of God are given us, so that we lay down all misery and tribulation on the congregation and "especially on Christ." "Though I am a sinner and have fallen, though this or that misfortune has befallen me, I will go to the sacrament to receive a sign from God that I have on my side Christ's righteousness, life and sufferings, with all the holy angels and all the blessed in heaven, and all pious men on earth." [4] What happens here is a kind of exchange. Christ receives us, takes upon himself our sins, and gives us his righteousness.

This theme pervades Luther's whole treatise. It is obvious that

[3] *WA* 2, 749; *PE* II, 19.
[4] *WA* 2, 745; *PE* II, 13.

he delights in expressing it in his vivid and vital language. The oft-quoted words in which Luther refers to the language of the *Didache* about the many grains made into one body are characteristic of his attitude. "Christ with all saints, by His love, takes upon Himself our form, fights with us against sin, death and all evil; this enkindles in us such love that we take His form, rely upon His righteousness, life and blessedness, and through the interchange of His blessings and our misfortunes are one loaf, one bread, one body, one drink, and have all things in common. This is a great sacrament, says Paul, that Christ and the church are one flesh and bone." [5]

These ideas in Luther's treatise are closely related to the *eschatological perspective*. The struggle against sin continues as long as life here on earth lasts. But when Christ is made manifest, we shall be like him. Luther bases this hope on the communion with Christ. "So complete is the fellowship of Christ and all the saints with us. . . . For this union makes all things common, until at last He completely destroys sin in us and makes us like unto Himself, at the last day." [6] Death separates us from everything visible; but in the sacrament the invisible and eternal things are given to us in order that we shall persevere in faith until we attain to them also by sight. Luther therefore likens the Lord's Supper to a ship "by which we pass from this world into eternal life." [7] Baptism leads us into a new life on earth; the bread guides us through death into eternal life. The two sacraments are associated with the Red Sea and the Jordan.

The result of Luther's method of presentation is an accentuation of the *eucharistic element*—the Lord's Supper as a service of joy and praise. When you realize, says Luther, that Christ and all his saints come to you in order to share everything with you, and when you exercise and strengthen this faith, "you will experience what

[5] *WA* 2, 748; *PE* II, 17, 18.
[6] *WA* 2, 749; *PE* II, 18, 19.
[7] *WA* 2, 753; *PE* II, 25.

a rich and joyous wedding-supper and festival your God has prepared upon the altar for you." [8] Luther refers in this connection to the statement in Acts that the apostles broke the bread and ate with great gladness of heart.

In addition to these eucharistic motifs there is one that plays a very important part in Luther's treatise. Again and again he insists that the *obligation of love* is inseparably connected with the sacrament. "Your heart must go out in love and devotion and learn that this sacrament is a sacrament of love, and that love and service are given you and you again must render love and service to Christ and His needy ones." [9] Jesus as Christ has given himself for us, so we must contend for the truth, prevent injustice, bear the misfortune and adversity of Christ and his saints. In this connection Luther attacked the current practice in the sacrifice of the mass which had neglected the example of Christ and forgotten the obligations of communion, "so that we hardly know what purpose this sacrament serves, or how it should be used, nay, with our masses we frequently destroy this fellowship and pervert everything. This is the fault of the preachers who do not preach the Gospel nor the sacrament, but their humanly devised fables." [10] Everything that Luther says about how the Lord's Supper obligates us to serve the neighbor is intimately connected with his fundamental point of view: if the Lord's Supper is communion, its effects must appear in the human context in which we stand. We cannot receive without a desire to give, "for the sacrament has no blessing and significance unless love grows daily and so changes a man that he is made one with all others." [11]

We must touch upon one more point in Luther's treatise, viz., the presence of Christ in the Lord's Supper. Luther maintains the real presence of the body and blood of Christ. This is indicated

[8] *WA* 2, 750; *PE* II, 20.
[9] *WA* 2, 745; *PE* II, 14.
[10] *WA* 2, 747; *PE* II, 16.
[11] *WA* 2, 749; *PE* II, 17.

even in the title. He even spoke at times of a change in the elements. But it is important to note the context in which this
expression occurs. "For just as the bread is changed into his true
natural body and the wine into his true natural blood, so truly
are we also drawn and changed into the spiritual body, that is, into
the fellowship of Christ and all saints, and put by this sacrament
in possession of all the virtues and mercies of Christ and his saints."
In this connection Luther points out the danger and the corruption
of the sacrament, if we are concerned only with "the natural" body
of Christ and regard the sacrament as an *opus operatum.* This
polemic against mechanization is directed against the sacrifice of the
mass. "Take heed; it is more needful that you discern the spiritual
than that you discern the natural body of Christ." [12] The whole
presentation indicates that the emphasis is on the fact that the
living Christ is actively present in the Lord's Supper and is received
in faith. In the Lord's Supper the exalted Christ, the Head of the
church which is his spiritual body, incorporates into his fellowship
whoever receives him in faith, and gives him a share in the riches
which he has secured. The background of all this is the finished
work of Christ. But the Lord's Supper itself is the continuous act of
the exalted Lord. He who once gave himself in death is the one
who gives himself for you, who makes your suffering and misfortune his own and bears them for you.[13]

We have now reviewed the most important ideas in Luther's
treatise of 1519. This story of the Lord's Supper is a thoroughly
religious document. It is fresh, filled with rich content, and free
from traditional scholasticism. The idea of communion pervades
the interpretation. What is of paramount importance is the communion with Christ and his spiritual body, the church; or we
could say, communion with Christ in his spiritual body. This
communion is realized in the sacrament through Christ who as the

[12] *WA* 2, 751; *PE* II, 22.
[13] *WA* 2, 745; *PE* II, 14.

Head of the church is present and active. To this communion motif Luther adds a number of others: the eschatological, the eucharistic, and the very important motif which we might call responsibility or stewardship, the obligation of willing service toward the neighbor.

The motif of sacrifice seems, however, to be completely absent. It is not dealt with directly, either positively or polemically. But the whole presentation is in sharp contrast to the contemporary practice in the sacrifice of the mass. The contrast appears already in the emphasis on the Lord's Supper as a communion. From the beginning the Reformers were intent on restoring communion to its rightful place in the celebration and to strive against the usage in the late Middle Ages which had replaced communion with contemplation of the sacrifice of the mass. The criticisms which appear from time to time in this writing are directed also against the mechanization of the Lord's Supper in the contemporary conceptions of the sacrifice of the mass.

The criticism of the sacrifice of the mass, which later became such an important matter to Luther, appears rather indirectly in this treatise. This is true also of Luther's positive attitude to the sacrifice. We may observe that both eucharistic praise and the obligation of serving the neighbor later on are referred to in terms of sacrifice both by Luther himself and in later Reformation theology. They speak of the sacrifice of thanksgiving and of willing sacrifice of service. The element which from the point of view of the theology of the Lord's Supper is most important, viz., the sacrifice of Christ, is not dealt with directly in the treatise. It is of course true that the sacrifice which Christ made once for all constitutes the background to everything that Luther has to say about the Lord's Supper. The sacrifice is present because the living Lord who meets us in the eucharist continually "gives himself for us" and "bears our burden." Only in passing does Luther refer to the words of institution as suggesting the sacrifice of death.

The reason we have dealt so much in detail with Luther's treatise of 1519 is due not only to the remarkable character of this writing, but also and above all to the fact that we meet here the original Reformation conception as it appeared before the great conflicts about the Lord's Supper during the decade of the 1520's. This writing is an important communion treatise and a Reformation document which must not be neglected. But if we are seeking for what became decisive in the later development within the Lutheran church of the Reformation, other documents claim our attention. Then Luther's catechisms become the chief witnesses. It is obvious that the instruction given here would assert the most far-reaching influence. The interpretation of the eucharist in the catechisms is not as broad and comprehensive as in the treatise of 1519, but is instead much more sharply delineated. The statements in the Small Catechism are positive rather than polemic, but it is quite obvious that they originated in connection with conflicts about the eucharist during the decade of the 1520's.

The presentation in the Small Catechism is concentrated in a few chief points. 1) With a reference to the words of institution Luther asserts that the sacrament of the altar "is the true Body and Blood of our Lord Jesus Christ, under the bread and wine, given to us Christians to eat and to drink, as it was instituted by Christ Himself." 2) The gift of Holy Communion, its "benefit," is defined as "remission of sins, life and salvation," for, he says, "where there is remission of sins, there is also life and salvation." 3) These great benefits of the eucharist are produced by the words, " 'Given and shed for you for the remission of sins.' For besides the bodily eating and drinking, these words are the chief thing in the Sacrament; and he who believes them has what they say and declare, namely, the remission of sins." Consequently Luther declares finally 4) that a right preparation for a worthy participation in the sacrament consists in believing these words.

This is all that the Small Catechism has to say about the Lord's

Supper, and the Large Catechism contains really nothing more than an exposition of these statements and an admonition to use the sacrament faithfully and frequently. There is, however, a certain complement to the words in the Small Catechism about the gift of the eucharist: it is given "for daily bread and food in order that faith may be restored and strengthened" during the struggle against the enemies of the new life.

Behind these formulations we can easily discern the points of conflict in the struggle about the Lord's Supper. The strong emphasis on the presence of the true body and blood of Christ is directed against Zwingli and "the fanatics [Schwärmer]." When he says that the "benefit" of the sacrament lies in the "gift" bestowed here, i.e., the gift of forgiveness of sins, he stresses his opposition to the sacrifice of the mass. When he says finally that "these great benefits" are not produced by "the eating and drinking," but through the words "given and shed for you for the remission of sins" embraced in faith, he rejects the idea of the sacrament as an *opus operatum.*

A comparison between the Small Catechism and the treatise of 1519 yields the following results. It is quite obvious that in the catechisms Luther bases his interpretation of Holy Communion entirely on the words of institution. Here he has discovered the exegetical basis for the real presence. In the Large Catechism we meet the same arguments which Luther used in his controversy with Zwingli—the literal interpretation of the words of Christ: This *is* my body. In the three other statements in the Small Catechism the words, "given and shed for you for the remission of sins," recur. These words interpret the gift of the Lord's Supper, impart it to the one who believes, and thereby clarify in what the true preparation consists.

If we compare the biblical evidence presented in the catechisms with the broad biblical basis found in the treatise of 1519, the difference appears very great. In the Catechism the repeated reference to the words "given" and "shed" places the emphasis on the act done once for all, the sacrifice on the cross. Consequently the idea of sacrifice is really more prominent in the catechism than in the treatise. The latter also speaks of his sacrifice in death. But what is most characteristic is the constantly recurring theme: how Christ the living Lord incorporates us into communion with himself, takes our burden upon himself, imparts his righteousness to us, and struggles with us and for us against the enemies of the new life.

The interpretation of Holy Communion in the catechisms has its center in the forgiveness of sins, but in his treatise Luther has concentrated his attention on the fellowship with "Christ and his saints" and the significance of this communion in the struggle against the enemies of the Christian life. Concentration on the forgiveness of sins involves no doubt a more definite formulation of the intention of the Reformation. But if we grant this, we must not transform this difference into a contradiction nor must we assume that later interpretations are to be identified with Luther himself. When he places the forgiveness of sins in the center, he intends to state that all fellowship and communion with God rest on this foundation and on no other. There is no other way to God than that which is opened through the gift of forgiveness. But this gift includes all other gifts. It cannot be overemphasized that in his interpretation of the eucharist Luther does not interpret forgiveness negatively as a remission of guilt, but positively as an incorporation into the family of God. The words "life and salvation" added to forgiveness indicate this positive meaning, and so also the direct statement: "for where there is forgiveness of sins, there is also life and salvation." The difference between the treatise of 1519 and the catechism is then that the former includes forgiveness in communion, while the latter establishes communion, with life and salvation, on the basis of forgiveness of sins. The situation became entirely different when in the later church the forgiveness of sins came to be interpreted from an exclusively negative point of view. Then there occurred a shrinking of the perspective which did not agree with Luther's intention; and which, when the eucharist was preceded by confession and absolution, caused uncertainty as to its significance.

But even if Luther's words about the gift of Holy Communion are allowed to retain the full meaning which they undoubtedly had for him, it cannot be denied that many of the eucharistic motifs which enriched his presentation in the treatise are lacking in the catechisms. The idea of communion has not been accentuated, nor does it stand in such intimate connection with the vivid conception of the church as the spiritual body of Christ which was so prominent in the older treatise. The eucharistic and the eschatological conceptions do not occur in the catechisms, nor is there the emphasis on the fact that Holy Communion involves an obligation to mutual service. This does not mean that Luther has abandoned or is opposed to such elements in the Lord's Supper; other writings on the subject indicate that this is not the case. Nevertheless it is unfortunate that in such tremendously influential books as the catechisms Luther did not present a more comprehensive conception of the Lord's Supper. We cannot justly maintain that the later decline can be traced to the limited presentation in the catechisms; the reasons are to be sought rather in later tendencies. But it must be said that these chief documents of the Reformation did not present an effective counterbalance to these tendencies, as, for instance the excessive individualism which has characterized later interpretations of the communion, nor against the gloomy aspect which the service later received. The reverence appeared in mourning and the eucharistic joy disappeared.

8

The Sacrifice

We have seen that the Reformation has been criticized from many sources because, in spite of whatever merits it may have had, it nevertheless in its polemic against Rome obscured the idea of sacrifice in the Lord's Supper and therefore lost something that was essential both for the ancient church and in the New Testament. Such accusations come not only from non-Lutheran sources but also from a theology which is strictly Lutheran in origin. Brilioth in his book, *Eucharistic Faith and Practice,* expresses regret that the approaches to a positive, evangelical conception of the sacrifice in the eucharist, which were present in Luther, were not developed either by him or in later Lutheran theology. The result was a suppression of "the memorial aspects" in the Supper.[1] Gustaf Wingren touches upon another side of the same matter. He suggests that the connection of the Holy Communion with mutual, human fellowship would have found a more prominent place "had not the deterioration of the idea of sacrifice through the sacrifice of the mass made Luther so excessively suspicious of any mention of sacrifice." The combination of liturgical and social elements which is found within Anglican piety "must be accepted as an ancient Christian heritage, which we Lutherans unfortunately have lost."[2]

It is undeniable that the idea of sacrifice occupies a very modest

[1] Brilioth, *op. cit.,* p. 140.
[2] Gustaf Wingren, *Predikan* (Lund, 1949), p. 229.

place within the Lutheran tradition. The development has been completely determined by Luther's polemical attitude, while his positive appreciation of the idea of sacrifice has left hardly any trace. There are, however, several indications that later theology has found this negative attitude unsatisfactory. Regin Prenter in his dogmatics, *Creation and Redemption,* has strongly emphasized the importance of the idea of sacrifice in the interpretation of the eucharist.[3] I might also be permitted to refer to my book, *The Faith of the Christian Church.* From the point of view of worship Peter Brunner gives the sacrifice a central place in his analysis of the eucharistic service.[4]

It is now necessary to enquire more fully into Luther's own attitude to the idea of sacrifice. In this discussion we will concentrate on two main points. 1) What was involved in Luther's struggle against the sacrifice of the mass and what were the religious interests at stake? 2) To what extent did Luther have a positive appreciation of the idea of sacrifice?

What was the main point in Luther's struggle against the sacrifice of the mass? Modern Roman theologians claim that Luther directed his criticism against corruptions, and that the golden thread through Augustine and Thomas represents an entirely different point of view from the one Luther attacked. Such an objection has a legitimate place in a modern discussion of Roman and Protestant theology. However, when we are trying to find what it was that caused Luther to engage in the conflict, there is no reason to discuss this problem. The situation which brought Luther into this struggle is not changed or improved by the fact that there were within the Roman tradition conceptions of better quality than those which Luther encountered during the sixteenth century.

Luther's criticism of the practice of the mass as it flourished

---

[3] Regin Prenter, *Skabelse og Genloesning* (Copenhagen, 1953), p. 511ff.
[4] Peter Brunner, "Zur Lehre vom Gottesdienst," *Leiturgia* (1954), p. 220ff.

in his day can be summed up by saying that it turned the gospel upside down. What was involved therefore, was not peripheral; it was a question of "the most precious treasure of the church." As is well known, Luther frequently said that the gospel was found in the church also "under the papacy." But in the sacrifice of the mass the gospel had been placed "under a bushel." The mass substitutes a "righteousness of works," "self-righteousness," for that righteousness which is given by grace alone.

We may elucidate the significance of his criticism by noting the following points. 1) Luther is opposed to the conception that the sacrifice of the mass should constitute a complementary sacrifice, whether it was assumed to be a repetition of the sacrifice on Golgotha or a new, additional sacrifice. 2) The sacrifice of the mass was given a meritorious significance. This was expressed both in the conception that the sacrifice on Golgotha atoned for deadly sins and the mass for venial sins, and in the performance of innumerable masses for the dead. 3) The offense is present already in the claim that the sacrifice in the eucharist is an offering of Christ performed by the officiating priest on behalf of the church. 4) This denial of the idea that Christ is brought forth as a sacrifice in the Lord's Supper leads to a criticism of the doctrine of transubstantiation, inasmuch as the miracle of the change was a necessary presupposition for the bringing of Christ's body and blood as a sacrifice. Luther rejected transubstantiation but maintained the real presence. What this involved we will have to discuss later.

When Luther criticizes the sacrifice of the mass at it was at that time proclaimed and practiced, he is concerned above all to assert that the mass stands in unreconcilable opposition to that act of reconciliation which Christ accomplished once for all and which was perfected in his death on the cross. This act of reconciliation need not and cannot be repeated or complemented by any new sacrifices. The mass denies the gracious act of Christ (*negat beneficium Christi*). It denies that the act which Christ has done once for all is sufficient and that the sacrifice he has made is eternally valid. Behind the sacrifice of the mass lurks the conception that God, even after Christ's act of atonement, remains the unreconciled God who must be propitiated by continued sacrifices.

What Luther wants to say is, therefore, that the sacrifice of the mass stands in conflict with the clear biblical message about the act of reconciliation which Christ has made once for all. The mass gives a false picture both of Christ's act of atonement and of God's relationship to it. It is necessary at this point to say a few words about the conception of the atonement which forms the background of and the basis for Luther's criticism of the eucharistic sacrifice. Luther conceives of Christ's act of atonement from two points of view. It is a struggle against and victory over "demonic forces," and it is also a vicarious sacrifice. The evil powers which are attacked and defeated are, according to Luther, sin, death, the devil, the law, and divine wrath. The idea of struggle and victory is everywhere prominent. We meet a classic example of Luther's line of thought in the *Commentary on Galatians* (1535): "So the curse, which is God's wrath against the whole world, came in conflict with the blessing, i.e., with God's eternal grace and mercy in Christ. The curse conflicts with the blessing and would bring it to nought, but cannot do so. For the blessing is divine and eternal, and therefore the curse must retreat. If the blessing in Christ could be overcome, then God himself also would be overcome. But this is impossible." [5] But this conception of struggle and victory does not stand in contradiction to the idea of sacrifice. The victory is won through suffering and self-oblation. Both in the act of struggle and victory and in the act of sacrifice God himself is present. The victory of the blessing over the curse is the victory of divine love. But the sacrifice, too, has a relationship to the activity of God. Christ offers himself. He goes the way of

[5] *WA* 40^I, 441ff.

sacrifice in obedience to his heavenly Father. From this point of view his sacrifice is an offering brought to God. But at the same time the love of the Father is the starting point of the sacrifice that is taking place: "God gave his only Son." He has finished the atonement. The victory has been won. The sacrifice is fulfilled and valid for ever.

In what relationship does this sacrifice of Christ stand to the Lord's Supper? It is obvious that we cannot speak of any complementary sacrifice on our part. Even apart from the fact that all human sacrifices are useless as an atonement, such claims would be blasphemy against the work of Christ and against God himself. "Justification" is forgiveness, and as such it is God's gift of grace alone for the sake of Jesus Christ. Nor can we speak of an offering of Christ. God has given, "offered" him, and he has offered himself unto death in obedience to the Father. But we cannot offer him. However, even though such ideas of sacrifice must be eliminated, it is clear that the eucharist is closely connected with the sacrifice of Christ and that it is totally dependent upon his act. The sacrifice of Christ is the presupposition and the foundation of the gift that is given in the eucharist, just as it is the foundation of the existence of the church. This connection between the Lord's Supper and the finished sacrifice of Christ is already expressed most clearly, as far as Luther is concerned, in the words of institution, "given and shed for you." This is clear beyond doubt. The question is whether Luther has anything to say in addition about the relationship between the sacrifice of Christ and the eucharist. In order to answer this question we must note the positive statements Luther has made in reference to the eucharistic sacrifice.

A review of Luther's treatment of this question reveals that his attitude toward the term "sacrifice" varied. In his earlier writings about the Lord's Supper prior to 1520 he employed the term quite frequently. But during the great controversy about the sacrament he seems deliberately to avoid speaking of sacrifice in connection with the eucharist. After 1530, however, the expression returns and occurs frequently thereafter in Luther's writings. We get the impression that the corruption of the idea of sacrifice in the doctrine of the mass caused Luther to avoid the use of the term for a while, but that sacrifice is such an integral part of the biblical record that the use of the word became unavoidable. It was natural that Luther should try to substitute a purified conception of sacrifice for the contemporary corruption of the idea. It was natural also that he should reject the doctrine of the eucharist as a propitiatory sacrifice and an offering up of Christ. "Christ has offered himself once for all; he does not will to be offered again by someone else."

We note here a few characteristic sayings about sacrifice and the Lord's Supper. In his "Treatise on the New Testament" (1520), Luther deals with this subject quite extensively. We are to offer ourselves, everything that we have, in fervent prayer. We are to offer wholehearted praise and thanksgiving for God's unspeakable grace and mercy. Two points of view expressed in this treatise are especially important. Referring to the high priestly service of Christ in heaven Luther says that we are to put ourselves upon Christ together with our sacrifice of prayer and praise. He brings them into the presence of God, "speaks and mediates for us." We observe that Luther here in a certain sense refers to a continuous sacrifice of Christ in heaven, and that in this connection he speaks of the mass as a sacrifice. "We do not offer Christ as a sacrifice, but Christ offers us. And in this way it is permissible, yea, profitable to call the mass a sacrifice, not on its own account, but because we offer ourselves as a sacrifice along with Christ; that is, we lay ourselves on Christ by a firm faith in His testament, and appear before God with our prayer, praise and sacrifice only through Him and through His mediation; and we do not doubt that He is our priest and minister in heaven before God. Such faith, forsooth, brings it to pass that Christ takes up our cause, presents us, our prayer and praise, and also offers Himself for us in heaven. If the

mass were so understood and therefore called a sacrifice, it would
be well. Not that we offer the sacrament, but that by our praise,
prayer and sacrifice we move Him and give Him occasion to offer
Himself for us in heaven, and ourselves with Him." Remarkably
enough Luther uses the expression, "offer Christ," in this exposition,
but he explains the significance immediately in order to avoid any
misunderstanding. Faith makes us all priests, he says, and in faith
"with the sacrament we offer ourselves, our need, prayer, praise and
thanksgiving in Christ and through Christ, and thereby offer Christ
before God, that is, give Him cause and move Him to offer Himself
for us and us with Himself." [6]

We turn now to a treatise of 1530 about the eucharist:
Vermahnung zum Sakrament des Leibs und Bluts unsers Herrn.
One of the main points in this writing is his concern to combine
the offering of praise with the remembrance and proclamation of
the death of Christ. Luther speaks as usual about the gift which
the eucharist bestows upon all who receive it in faith. But the sacrifice of praise, which he emphasizes so strongly here, is not only the
individual person's thanksgiving and praise for the gift which he
has received. The sacrament as such is a gift, not a sacrifice. But
to use the sacrament is already in itself a sacrifice of praise which
confers on Christ the honor which belongs to him. Luther speaks
of two ways of honoring him. The first consists in not despising
God's institution and ordinance, but rather using them willingly.
"The other honor is to keep and maintain the remembrance of
Christ. It is to proclaim, praise and give thanks for the grace of
Christ bestowed on us poor sinners, for whose sake God has especially
instituted this sacrament, and in this seeks and demands such honor
in order that we in Christ may learn to know and acknowledge our
God." [7]

These words indicate that when Luther talks about the sacrifice

[6] *WA* 6, 368ff; *PE* I, 294, 314ff.
[7] *WA* 30[II], 614.

of praise connected with the eucharist, he does not have in mind only the thanksgiving of the individual Christian, as has been frequently claimed. The offering of praise is rather something that is connected with and demanded by the institution of the sacrament. It belongs to the proclamation of the death of Christ and magnifies his perfect act of reconciliation.

If we are to try to obtain a general view of what Luther has said about the eucharistic sacrifice, we must differentiate between two kinds of sacrifices. On the one hand, we are dealing with the "offering" which we, or the church, bring, and, on the other hand, with Christ's offering of himself. In regard to the former we find that Luther uses this expression in various connections. He speaks often of how we bring our need, our sin, and our suffering as a "sacrifice." Such points of view are congenial to his thinking. Nothing could be more foreign to him than that the "offering" which we bring to God should possess any kind of "merit." At this point Luther directed his most violent and unrelenting attack against the conceptions he found connected with the sacrifice of the mass.

The ideas of sacrifice which Luther otherwise connects with the eucharist are, as we have seen, praise, prayer, and willing service. None of Luther's many writings about the Lord's Supper accentuates the obligation to mutual service inherent in the eucharist as does the treatise of 1519. Here there is a direct line from the principal motif of communion to human, social life. As Christ carries our burden so we are to bear one another's burdens. It must be said that this aspect of the celebration of the Lord's Supper appears infrequently in Luther's later eucharistic writings. Naturally this does not mean that Luther has rejected the claim of service to the neighbor, or that he now regards it as of lesser importance. Luther's view of the Christian calling testifies to the contrary. Nevertheless we must regard it as a loss that this emphasis on the social perspective has lost its connection with the eucharist. As a result the communion motif was weakened. This had an influence on later development and contributed to the emergence of a one-sided individualistic interpretation of the Lord's Supper.

Prayer and intercession is for Luther something essential in worship life. Prayer is an approach to Christ, for in him man meets God. Christ is the altar, says Luther, on which the one who prays is offered, and through which our prayers appear before God. It is natural, therefore, that "the offering of prayer" should belong to the celebration of the eucharist. But this perspective is not as prominent as we might expect. We find here a certain restraint, and the offering of praise is much more in evidence than the offering of prayer. Vilmos Vajta points out that the reason for this was Luther's opposition to the conception that the sacramental rite made the prayers offered in the mass effective.[8] The restraint is connected with his criticism of the common Medieval practice in the mass. He who used the mass in this way, says Luther, was concerned only with himself. When the thankfulness for God's gift had found its due place in the offering of praise, then only could the offering of prayer be rightly used.

Luther has consequently found a secure place for the sacrifice of praise in the celebration of the sacrament. It belongs to the institution of the sacrament and is a part of its essence. To celebrate the eucharist is to bring thanksgiving and praise to Christ and to give to him the honor which belongs to him. The subject of praise is especially the death of Christ. It might seem strange at first that the eucharistic element has been connected with the death of Christ. A strong emphasis on Holy Communion as a commemoration of the death of Christ has often tended to eliminate the eucharistic element and has given a somber character to the celebration. This happened frequently in later Lutheran history. But Luther himself looked at this differently. The death on the cross

[8] Vilmos Vajta, *Luther on Worship* (Philadelphia: Muhlenberg, 1958), p. 161ff.

signified that the act of sacrifice was finished; it included the victory and the completion of the work of redemption. The Lord's Supper becomes then a celebration of the finished work of redemption and of the unfathomable mercy of God in Christ.

There is no doubt but that Luther wanted to preserve the eucharistic element in the Lord's Supper. The liturgies which he produced testify to this desire. Although in his criticism of the mass he radically attacked the Roman canon, because here "almost everything suggests sacrifice," he preserved the song of praise in his *Formula missae.* When later he substituted German paraphrases for the Latin hymns of praise in his *Deutsche Messe,* it was not his intention to reduce the element of praise in the celebration. As an indication of the opposite intention we may point out that Luther's evangelical chorals of praise sounded forth the eucharistic element in the celebration of the Lord's Supper.

We proceed now to the question of the relationship between the sacrifice of Christ and the eucharist. We have already time and again referred to this question. We have seen that the sacrifice on Golgotha is the foundation on which all celebration of the eucharist rests; that the sacrifice of praise and of prayer is intimately connected with the sacrifice of Christ, not only as something done once for all but as a continuous act of the heavenly High Priest. There are, however, many questions remaining unanswered. In our attempt to answer these and at the same time define Luther's point of view more accurately it is necessary to consider Luther's conception of the real presence. It will become clear that the questions about the real presence and the relationship of the sacrifice of Christ to the eucharist are inseparably connected.

9

Sacrifice and the Real Presence

It is obvious that we cannot speak of Luther's teaching of the Lord's Supper without speaking about the real presence. To maintain that Christ was really present in the eucharist was one of Luther's most vital concerns. His view is even today spoken of as consubstantiation. In using this term the intention is to indicate Luther's twofold opposition: against the spiritualism of Zwingli and the "fanatics," and against the Roman doctrine of transubstantiation. That there was such a twofold opposition is undeniable. But it is questionable whether this term consubstantiation, which was taken over from medieval theology, and which Luther did not use, clearly expresses the essential point in Luther's teaching. In reality it does not at all express what is characteristic in Luther's conception of the presence of Christ in the eucharist; rather it draws the attention away from that which was essential in his thinking.

Luther's doctrine of the real presence has both an exegetical and a christological point of reference. Exegetically the important passage is that containing the words of institution. When Luther at Marburg maintained the real presence of the body and blood of Christ in the bread and the wine, he referred to the words of institution: "this is." We need not discuss here the validity of this exegesis. But we must point out that Luther repeatedly declared that he was bound to this *hoc est.* The title of his treatise on the Lord's Supper against the fanatics, of 1527, bears witness to this fact: *Dass diese Worte Christi "Das ist mein Leib" noch fest stehen, wider die Schwarmgeister.*

But Luther's thinking on the real presence has also a christological point of reference. We encounter here his doctrine of ubiquity. What is the intention of this christological reference? It is not to explain *how* Christ is present in the bread and the wine. All such speculations were foreign to Luther. But he wanted to indicate the basis on which the real presence depends. As is well known, he referred to the *communicatio idiomatum,* the intercommunication of the properties of the divine and human natures of Christ. Since the human nature participates in the omnipresence of the divine nature, the ascended and exalted Christ is present everywhere. "The right hand of God is everywhere."

The attempt might readily be made to place the exegetical reference over against the christological, and thus suggest two different modes of presence. In one case we would think of the historical past, the body which once was offered on the cross; in the other case we would be concerned with the living, glorified Lord who makes his presence known. In one case it is an impersonal, bodily presence; in the other, a personal, spiritual presence. But by such a division we would not understand Luther's intention at all. He would ask with Paul: Is Christ divided? In both cases it is one and the same Christ, *totus Christus,* at the same time the one crucified and glorified. It is the glorified Christ, the one "everywhere present," who, according to his word, has connected his presence with the bread and the wine, and who thereby *actualizes his sacrifice and makes it present.*

If we are to understand Luther's intentions correctly, we must analyze his doctrine of the real presence in both of these aspects. In the history of theology Luther's doctrine of the Lord's Supper has been subject to misinterpretations either in a grossly materialistic or a vaguely spiritual sense.

In his reference to Christology Luther maintains that the exalted,

living Christ is present everywhere, but that, according to his own
word, he has connected his redemptive presence in the eucharist—
"for you"—to the bread and the wine. Christ is present, not because
he is compelled to be in any way through the eucharistic rite, but
because of his own sovereign power and according to his own
promise.

This conception is opposed both to the doctrine of transubstantiation and to the theory that Christ's body is completely localized in
heaven. From the days of the ancient church theology labored with
the idea of substance, the ontology of substance. The incarnation
was conceived of as a union of human and divine "substance." On
the presupposition of this theology of substance the Medieval
church arrived at the doctrine of transubstantiation; and from the
same starting point Zwingli insisted on localizing the substance of
Christ in heaven. The real significance of Luther's doctrine of
ubiquity lies in the fact that he broke away from this dilemma.
In spite of the scholastic elements which still remain in this doctrine
of ubiquity, he has freed himself through it from the scholastic
alternative of localizing Christ in the one way or the other, which
was inseparably connected with the ontology of substance. But
Luther's work of liberation has often been obscured and destroyed
by his theological successors. During the period of Orthodoxy the
most fantastic speculations were connected with the "Lutheran"
doctrine of ubiquity. It was asserted, for instance, that the blood
of Christ which was poured out on the cross was taken up again
into his glorified body at the resurrection in order that it might be
present in the eucharistic wine. With such absurd speculations,
which have been repeated even in later times, Luther's intentions
have been completely misinterpreted, and preposterous answers
have been given to senseless and irrelevant questions. Such "interpretations of Luther" we may ignore completely. But we must
retain what was essential in his argumentation; namely, that the
living and glorified Lord, who is exalted above all limitations of

time and space, has according to his promise connected his redemptive presence in the eucharist with the bread and the wine.

From this point of view what is the significance of this real presence in the bread and wine? We must affirm first of all that Luther definitely connected the eucharistic gift with the real presence. He did not make a distinction between the spiritual reception of the eucharistic gift and the bodily eating and drinking, as if these were two different matters. On the contrary, these two "receptions" are inseparably connected. The bread and wine are the external means through which the eucharistic gift is bestowed. The reason why Luther conceived of the matter in this way becomes clearly evident in his reckoning with the spiritualistic interpretation of the eucharist. It is essential for him that the gift is given in a tangible and visible manner, so that it becomes clear that it is really a gift and not only thoughts which we may have during the celebration. If we despise the fact that the gift comes to us in this external form, it indicates that we have a conception of anamnesis as a mere recollection of the absent Lord and his redemptive act in the past. In this way the gift itself becomes obscured. All that is left are the thoughts called forth by the symbolic signs of the eucharist. But Luther states: "The Lord does not say: your thoughts about me are in me, or my thoughts are in you; but rather, you are in me and I am in you." [1] In virtue of the presence of Christ the external things, bread and wine, are the vehicles of the spiritual gift. To receive it thus in faith is rightly to commune at the Lord's table.

Against the background of these ideas of Luther's we can now define more accurately the significance of the real presence in the bread and the wine. The exalted Christ makes known his presence in bread and wine. In this way the identity between the glorified and living Christ and the Christ who gave himself on the cross is revealed. In reality everything points to this sacrifice which is

[1] *WA* 33, 225, quoted by Prenter, *op. cit.*, p. 533.

the starting point and the presupposition of the eucharistic gift
and communion with Christ. What happens through the real
presence in bread and wine is that the living Christ actualizes his
eternally valid sacrifice and makes it into an *effectively present
reality*. This is the essential significance of the real presence. The
presence is possible because Christ lives glorified "at the right hand
of God." That the presence is realized in the eucharistic bread and
wine means that his perfect sacrifice is made present. The presence
of the body and blood of Christ in the bread and wine is the presence
of his sacrifice. We must not be misled by the fact that Luther
does not use the word sacrifice in this connection. The word does
not occur but the idea is there. It is not only there, but it is the
most essential element. The sacrifice of Christ perfected in his
death is not merely something that happened once in the past. It
is a sacrifice that is valid for all time and all generations, and it is
realized in the living present when the glorified Lord connects his
presence in the eucharist with the bread and wine.

One of the Swedish reformers, Laurentius Petri, speaks of the
eucharist as a "representation" of the sacrifice of Christ. "If you
would call the sacrament a sacrifice because it signifies and represents the sacrifice which Christ made once on the cross, and not,
as you now do, ascribe to it or to the priests the office of Christ
himself, then I might very well admit that you may designate it as
a sacrifice." [2] The expression which the Swedish reformer used,
representatio, has been much discussed lately by Lutheran theologians. Peter Brunner writes that the sacrifice perfected on the
cross becomes present in the eucharistic bread and wine. "Through
the real presence of the body and blood of Jesus Christ the
representatio which takes place in the eucharist receives its concrete
manifestation." [3] One critic has objected that the term italicized

[2] Quoted by Brilioth, *op. cit.* (Swed. ed.), p. 360 (not in English trans.).
[3] Brunner, *op. cit.*, p. 238.

by Brunner himself ought not to be used in evangelical theology; it originated in scholasticism and it invites false associations.[4]

But the expressions which cannot lead to "false associations" are very few in number. Aside from that, however, it is undeniable that the term rightly interpreted expresses a point of view which is genuinely and essentially Lutheran. If it is said that the eucharist, the bread and wine, signifies or represents the sacrifice of Christ, the expression would certainly be too weak if understood merely in a symbolic sense. The important thing is that we are concerned here with a "sign" or a "re-presentation" which includes the reality itself. The presence of Christ in bread and wine is the effective presence of his sacrifice. The effect manifests itself in the eucharistic gift. Under all circumstances we must maintain that the presence here discussed is realized by Christ himself and not by someone else. Christ is the one who acts and works. It therefore becomes clearer if we speak of his presence rather than of his re-presentation. If Christ is present there is no need of his being "represented."

After this discussion of terminology we return to the idea of sacrifice which, as far as Luther is concerned, is included in the real presence. We must now explain a little more fully what significance his twofold point of reference, the exegetical and the christological, has for his conception of the eucharist. The words of institution direct our attention to the Crucified, to the sacrifice on the cross; the christological reference directs our attention to the risen, glorified Lord. It is extremely important that these two aspects are kept together. Without this synthesis Luther's interpretation of the Lord's Supper disintegrates into disparate fragments. His deepest intentions would be lost. If we look at the history of the doctrine of the eucharist in the Lutheran churches, we cannot escape the impression that the synthesis has often been obscured

[4] Vilmos Vajta in *Svensk Teologisk Kvartalskrift* (*Swedish Theological Quarterly*), 1955, p. 65.

or lost altogether. This has happened mostly because the attention
has been one-sidedly directed toward the death on the cross. This
explains why the celebration of the eucharist has often received a
mournful character. In this case we have held fast to Luther's
formula of the real presence but without realizing its full meaning.
That situation has not been rectified by substituting as a reaction
an emphasis on the heavenly Christ. That way we arrive at a
purely spiritualistic interpretation of the sacrament far removed
from Luther's intention.

In reality it is the synthesis of the living and crucified Christ
which determines Luther's interpretation of the eucharist. The
living Christ appears in action. But when he realizes his presence
in the eucharist, it occurs in and with the bread and wine. This
means that the living Lord is none other than the Crucified who
now actualizes his sacrifice, makes this eternally valid sacrifice a
factor in the present, and thereby also makes those who receive the
elements participants in his sacrificial act of love and partakers
of its fruits. This synthesis of the crucified and the living One, of
cross and resurrection, illuminates the gift which is given in the
eucharist. We understand why Luther in his Small Catechism
combines "the forgiveness of sins" with "life and salvation," and
why we find him also having that conception of the gift which
expressed itself in the way in which the ancient church spoke of
the eucharist as "the medicine of immortality." The eucharist is
food on the way to the new life of the resurrection. Sacrifice and
victory belong inextricably together. The sacrifice of Christ in
death *is* victory, the victory that led to the resurrection. Consequently the participation in the sacrifice of Christ which the
eucharist mediates signifies also a participation in the resurrection,
an anticipation of the life that is to come. The eschatological
perspective is inseparately connected with the eucharist.

The real presence of which Luther speaks means, as we have
seen, a presence of the eternally valid sacrifice made once for all.

But the One who is present is the living and glorified Christ, the one who acts. It is he who in this way actualizes his sacrifice in the eucharist. This point of view involves certain consequences which must be noted lest we misunderstand his whole conception.

In the first place, if it is Christ himself who makes the sacrifice of his body and blood a present reality in the eucharist, it is obvious that the real presence cannot be brought about by any effort on our part. It cannot be produced by the officiating priest on the basis of some power granted to him. Luther attaches the real presence closely to the words of institution. The celebrating congregation is to obey the admonition of the Lord: "Do this in remembrance of me." The Formula of Concord correctly interprets Luther's words here when it says that this command embraces "the whole eucharistic action, so that at this Christian gathering we take bread and wine, bless, distribute, receive, eat and drink them, and thereby proclaim the Lord's death." But that the real presence occurs depends entirely "on the power of almighty God and on the word, institution and order of our Lord Jesus Christ." The Formula of Concord refers here to two statements by Luther. "Not our word and action, but the command and direction of Christ make the bread into his body and the wine into his blood." "When according to his direction and command we say in the eucharist, 'this is my body,' it is his body, not because of our word or power, but because he has instructed us to say and do this and has connected his command and his action with our words." [5] According to Luther "the consecration" is bound up with the words of institution, which are at the same time interpretive words.

In the second place, if Christ is the one who makes his sacrifice present in the Lord's Supper, the idea that we should offer Christ is excluded. Here is the sharpest division between Luther and the doctrine of the mass which he attacked. The real presence

[5] Cf. *WA* 38, 240; 26, 285.

means that the sacrifice of Christ is present in the eucharist, but this presence is completely the work of Christ. He has once for all perfected that sacrifice which no one else can make, and now he actualizes it and its results in the sacrament. We have no control over him and his sacrifice, as if it were a gift which we could present to God in order to become reconciled to him. The sacrifice is the gift of Christ, not our gift. Regin Prenter has presented very clearly how the Lord's Supper is "the eternal presence in the church of the sacrifice on Golgotha." But he is not in agreement with the conception of the Lutheran Reformation when he writes: "We must say that in the eucharist we do not only present the elements and our prayers as a sacrificial offering, but also the body and blood of Jesus, which is the only gift of love we can present." [6] Such a statement somehow removes the sacrifice from the act of Christ and conceals the fact that in the eucharist, too, Christ is the living and active Lord. In reality the doctrine of transubstantiation (which of course Prenter does not accept) is the only basis for the suggestion that we offer Christ or his body and blood. Such a conception of the sacrifice is perfectly consistent with the doctrine of the change taking place in the elements, but it cannot be held after this doctrine has been rejected.

The distinction we make here is of fundamental significance for the clarification of the Lutheran interpretation of the eucharist. We must not be misled by the fact that in the literature of the Reformation we find statements like this one from the Swedish reformer, Laurentius Petri: the Lord's Supper may be called a sacrifice "because the priest and the congregation interpose it between the wrath of God and their sins as a sign of peace." The meaning of such a statement is not that we present Christ as an atoning sacrifice, but rather that we trust in his sacrifice alone. We who stand under the wrath of God because of our sins find in his sacrifice the God of reconciliation, mercy, and forgiveness. In

[6] Prenter, *op. cit.*, p. 515.

this sense the sacrifice of Christ is "a sign of peace." Laurentius Petri makes it very clear that it is not a question about an atoning sacrifice brought by us. The discussion, says he, is not whether the Lord's Supper "may in some sense be called a sacrifice. Our objection is to the wrong conception you have when you say that the priests make an offering for sin, and thus you reject, deny, and blaspheme the real sacrifice of Christ. . . . If you put away such wrong thoughts and opinions, I will not object if you call the mass a sacrifice." [7]

Finally we must consider whether Luther conceived of the sacrifice of Christ as finished or continuous. In the *Treatise on the New Testament* (1520), with reference to the high priestly service of Christ in heaven, Luther says that Christ speaks and mediates for us, that he is our priest who receives us, brings our prayers and praise and ourselves before God, and gives himself for us in heaven. Even if such direct statements about a continuous sacrifice of Christ are not numerous, it is one of the fundamental conceptions of Luther that Christ continues his redemptive work in that he assumes our burden and is our spokesman before God. Even though Luther at times may use the term sacrifice in this connection, he does assert with great emphasis that the sacrifice which began when Christ emptied himself and became man was finished on the cross. The sacrifice which occurred once for all, and which is eternally valid, neither can nor needs to be complemented.

It might appear that there is a certain contradiction between these two points of view, but it is only an apparent one. The contradiction is dissolved by the fact that sacrifice is used in two different senses. The sacrifice which is fulfilled and finished is the atoning sacrifice. This has been made once for all. It was God who in Christ reconciled the world to himself. The atonement is eternally valid. But the redemptive work of Christ continues through

---

[7] Quotation in Brilioth, *op. cit.* (Swed. ed.), p. 360 (not in English trans.).

all ages and generations. This activity rests on the finished act of reconciliation and involves a continuous realization of the reconciliation which has been won. "The sacrifice" of which we may speak in this connection is not an atoning sacrifice, but an expression of the indissoluble union between Christ and his church. The continuous, "high priestly" sacrifice testifies that the new life of the church issues from the life of Christ; it is supported by Christ and is a life "in Christ."

Here we must close our study of the sacrificial motif in Luther's interpretation of the Lord's Supper. We have seen that the idea of sacrifice is found frequently in his writings. In various contexts he speaks of a sacrifice on our part: a sacrifice of praise, prayer, and mutual service. But this is not the central idea. All such "sacrifices" are of secondary significance. The only real and fully valid sacrifice is the sacrifice of Christ himself. In reality everything that Luther has to say in his interpretation of the eucharist revolves around this one sacrifice which was finished once for all on the cross, but which nevertheless is present in its eternal validity in the eucharist. Luther's insistence on the real presence is a witness to this fact. On the basis of this sacrifice we are permitted to bring our sin and guilt to him and to receive the gift of forgiveness. Everything that may be called a sacrifice rests on this same sacrifice of Christ.

The claim has been made both within and outside of the Lutheran church that the idea of sacrifice has found no place in Luther's interpretation of the Lord's Supper. Is this really true? Others, as for instance Vajta, maintain that everything Luther did was intended to let sacrifice regain its biblical significance in the worship life of the church.[8] Luther did not neglect the idea of sacrifice; he only desired to give it a different place from the one it had in Roman theology. Is this true? Neither one of these questions can be answered with a simple yes or no. We have seen

[8] Vajta, *Luther on Worship*, p. 151.

that the conception of sacrifice is preserved in Luther's teaching
of the Lord's Supper, and that in reality it plays a very important
part. But at the same time it is evident that we encounter in his
works a certain reserve and moderation in regard to the word
"sacrifice." This is due to his reaction against the misuse of the
word in the contemporary doctrine and practice of the mass. The
result was that the sacrificial motif appears in Luther under the
disguise of a different terminology. This is true in regard to all
the different meanings of sacrifice. It is especially true in regard
to the sacrifice of prayer and of mutual service, but to a relatively
lesser extent in the case of the sacrifice of praise. But most especially is it true in regard to the sacrifice of Christ himself. In
this case the real presence becomes equivalent to the presence of
his sacrifice. The result of this attitude was that Luther's treatment of the sacrifice of the mass took the form of criticism rather
than a positively developed teaching about the sacrifice in the
eucharist. Luther's ideas about this matter are indeed biblical. But
he has not presented a direct, positive doctrine of sacrifice. This
attitude naturally influenced later Lutheran theology and contributed to the neglect of the sacrificial motif in the Lord's Supper.
This development finds apparent but no real support in Luther.

10

A Picture From the Late
Nineteenth Century

Before we close this section on the Reformation, we shall examine
how the Lord's Supper was understood and celebrated four hun-
dred years after the Reformation in a church which owed its reformation to the influence of Luther. We cannot, of course, follow
the development of the Lutheran conception of the sacrament
through the centuries. That would be too lengthy, and it is also
for our purpose unnecessary. But, on the contrary, it may be important to draw a quick picture from a later time. There is a
special reason for doing this because we have directed our presentation toward the ecumenical discussion of the eucharist. The fact
is that some ecumenical debaters judge the Reformation on the
basis of the situation in the churches which belong to a much
later date. As we move from the Reformation to the late nineteenth century, it is not our intention to present a detailed survey
of the position of the Lord's Supper in the various Lutheran
churches. We limit ourselves to a description of the situation in
the Church of Sweden. In doing so we are clearly conscious of
the fact that the picture may not accurately present the situation
in other Lutheran communions.

We may first say a few words about the place of the celebration of the Lord's Supper in the worship life. Its position about the
turn of the century was rather precarious, weaker than in any of

the other parts of the Lutheran church. Both the frequency of celebration and the number of communicants were rapidly declining. The service without the celebration of the Lord's Supper was regarded as normal. This did not at all agree with what Luther had intended and struggled for with his admonition to frequent participation in communion. It is true that his and the Reformation's efforts in this direction always have met with difficulties. One reason for this was the Reformation demand that the eucharist should never be celebrated without communion. It was of course vastly easier to arrange for masses without communion than to gather the members of the congregation to frequent communions. But from Luther's point of view these masses without communion were no sign that the eucharist enjoyed the prominent place it ought to have in the worship life of the church, but rather the opposite.

When in later time the sacrament lost this central position, the reasons for this development were varied. It was due partly to the conception of the means of grace which gradually became dominant. From the days of the Reformation the two forms of the means of grace were the Word and the sacraments. Luther's discovery, or rediscovery, of the Word as a means of grace was something new in relation to Medieval tradition. When Thomas Aquinas in his *Summa* explains how salvation is transmitted to men, he refers to the sacraments without mentioning the preaching of the Word. But no matter how strongly Luther maintains that the full gospel confronts us in the proclamation of the Word, this emphasis in no sense involved a minimizing of the sacrament. The grace of God which the means of grace impart is one and indivisible. Whenever this grace is given to man, it is given fully and completely, not in parts or in variously important quantities. The relationship between Word and sacrament is not a matter of different rating. Such a position was entirely foreign to Luther. He never warns against overestimating the sacrament. He is rather always concerned to maintain that the sacrament is a real means of grace—both against Rome and against the "fanatics." His struggle against the contemporary doctrine and practice of the mass was caused by his conviction that this represented a depreciation of the sacrament as a means of grace.

This view of the Word and the sacrament obtained in general in the period of orthodoxy. We are aware, however, of a terminological shift when the sacrament is referred to as "a visible Word." Such an expression might indicate that the sacrament is something secondary in reference to the Word. This might result in posing the question of relative importance, which did not exist as far as the Reformation was concerned.

When we come to the pietistic movements, it is evident that here the question of rank was present, consciously or unconsciously, and that this question was answered to the disadvantage of the sacrament. The Lord's Supper now becomes treasured as a special expression of the mutual and relatively exclusive fellowship of believers, and at the same time also as a confessional act. When these points of view become dominant, the idea of a means of grace is minimized. To the extent that it is preserved at all, the eucharist becomes a secondary means of grace in comparison with the Word. We need hardly add that later on the theology of the Enlightenment, in so far as it influenced the worship life, led to a minimizing and a setting aside of the sacrament.

Not only these general movements but also special factors served to impair the position of the sacrament in the Church of Sweden during the nineteenth century. One of these factors was that the Lord's Supper had gradually become in a sense a legal institution. In order to enjoy fully the privileges of congregational as well as civil citizenship it was necessary to commune at least once a year. Regulations of this kind were established by the church law of 1686 and remained in effect until the middle of the nineteenth century. This legalistic view of the Lord's Supper involved a great handicap. It was natural that participation in the eucharist came to be regarded as a mere formality. These legal requirements exercised a baneful influence even long after they had been removed.

It was inevitable that attendance at the Lord's Supper should diminish when coercion was finally removed. This tendency was accelerated under the influence of pietistic conceptions of what constituted a "worthy" guest at the table of the Lord. The watchword, "pure tables," became frequently used. The guest at the Lord's Table ought to be properly qualified. We need hardly say that this conception of "worthiness" is radically different from what Luther says on this subject, for example, in his Large Catechism. In so far as these ideas became popular, they helped to keep the people away from the Lord's table. The intention was good, but they contradicted the conception of unmerited grace and did not pay sufficient attention to the word of the gospel: "this man receives sinners and eats with them."

How did the celebration of the Lord's Supper appear at the end of the nineteenth century? What was the common conception of the significance of the eucharist? These questions are relatively easy to answer, especially by one who like the author has clear memories from this time.

We must first say that the Lutheran celebration of the Lord's Supper always has had, and even at that time did have its principal strength in deep seriousness and reverent quietness—a great asset which is well worth preserving. Whatever thoughts we have had about the Lord's Supper, the sacrament has always appeared as an inscrutable mystery, which contained the whole fulness of the secret of salvation. But the generation that knelt at the eucharistic table during the last decades of the nineteenth century regarded the eucharist more as a *mysterium tremendum* than a *mysterium fascinosum*.

We had learned from Luther's Small Catechism that the eucharistic gift consists in the forgiveness of sins. This viewpoint had been more thoroughly impressed upon the people than any other.

But this did not mean that they followed Luther's intentions completely. He had spoken of the eucharistic gift as "forgiveness of sins, life and salvation." The emphasis was placed much more on "the forgiveness of sins" than on "life and salvation." The preparatory confessional service which was combined with the celebration of the eucharist contributed greatly to this emphasis. This meant that forgiveness of sins came to be regarded simply as remission of guilt in a negative rather than positive sense. The conception appeared very clear but one-sided.

On closer examination it appears, however, that the matter was not so very clear. The celebration was preceded by the confessional service which closed with the absolution. If then the forgiveness of sin was bestowed already in the preceding service through the absolution, the question would arise as to what the specific gift bestowed in the eucharist really is. It is understandable that the emphasis could be placed, and in reality often was placed, on the introductory action. To attend the celebration of the Lord's Supper was "to go to confession." The eucharist could easily be regarded as a duplication of or an appendix to the confessional service with absolution. Was the eucharist a confirmation of the gift already received? Or might it be that since the absolution was conditional, the eucharist provided greater security? No definite answer could be given to such questions. Such questions were in the air, as it were; but they were not specifically asked and much less answered.

Another characteristic feature in the conception of the eucharist at that time was the strongly individualistic orientation. The eucharist and its gift were regarded exclusively from the point of view of the individual communicant. In agreement with the Reformation all held that the eucharist should not be celebrated without communion. But that did not mean that the attention was drawn to the communion motif, and still less that they had any appreciation of its rich and varied content. The vivid picture of the many facets of fellowship which Luther had painted in his treatise of 1519 had lost its bright colors. The one-sided, individualistic orientation had a certain connection with the negative interpretation of forgiveness. The perspective would no doubt have been widened and deepened if the positive aspect, "life and salvation," had been more strongly accentuated. The background of this individualism was the impoverished conception of the church which since the period of Pietism had obtained in the churches of the Reformation.

If we now ask how this development is related to the Reformation, the answer would have to be that this is not really a "development" but rather a departure caused by entirely different factors from those associated with the Reformation. The Lutheran Reformation was not individualistic. The conception of the church was always a living and self-evident reality. But because it was self-evident, it was seldom emphasized in the interpretation of the eucharist. Luther's treatise of 1519 was a brilliant exception. This omission did not cause any serious consequences during the period of the Reformation when the consciousness of living in the church was very vivid. When the situation changed, it became a serious matter that the communion motif had not found a proper place in the documents which had such great influence in later history as, for instance, Luther's catechisms. To that extent we may say that the Reformation contributed to a departure in the direction of individualism. Or, to state it more exactly: it could not effectively prevent the development in the interpretation of the eucharist which was caused by other factors than those present in the Reformation.

What we have already said about the celebration of the Lord's Supper toward the end of the nineteenth century indicates that the eucharistic element could not have been very prominent. The dominant position of the confessional service, the negative interpretation of forgiveness and the one-sided individualism indicate that the Lord's Supper could not have been regarded as the church's great act of thanksgiving and praise. There was the proper serious reverence. But the joy which shines forth in the celebration of the sacrament in the ancient church was not there, or at least was rather suppressed. The sacrament was dressed in black. The atmosphere was that of Good Friday rather than Easter. The eucharistic liturgy during the nineteenth century was the poorest the Swedish church has ever had. There was naturally something left of the great texts of praise from the ancient church. But these were very few, and the hymns were in a minor key.

After we have noted that the celebration had to a great extent lost the eucharistic joy, we must ask what had caused this development. There were very good reasons for this situation. If the atmosphere was that of Good Friday, it meant that the death of Christ was the dominant element. The death on the cross was the presupposition for the gift of forgiveness bestowed in the sacrament. As the service was conducted it was designed to emphasize the redemptive act accomplished on the cross. The Pauline words of the eucharist as a "proclamation of the Lord's death" stood as a superscription over the sacrament. But the added words, "until he comes," were not regarded as relevant. Nor was attention drawn to the living Christ. To be sure, they held with Luther to the real presence of Christ in the bread and the wine. But they had severed the threads which had tied the real presence to the living and active Lord. They had forgotten what Luther had intended with his doctrine of ubiquity, and they regarded this doctrine merely as a peculiar scholastic speculation. When the real presence thus ceased to stand in relationship to the living and active Lord, thinking began to be concerned with the function of the bread and the wine and what happened to them. They became concerned with the question of locality which Luther had sought to avoid. In reality the "Lutheran" doctrine of the real presence, understood as "consubstantiation," inevitably appeared as a variant form of the Roman doctrine of transubstantiation. They knew that this should be rejected, but they did not really know what this rejection involved. In general there developed a feeling of uncertainty in regard to the Lutheran doctrine of the real presence. It is not strange that this happened. It was a natural result of the fact that the mystery had been separated from the context in which it was meaningful without on that account ceasing to be a mystery. When the profound sense of meaning had been lost, the whole complex became simply obscure talk. From this point of view, too, it is understandable that the mystery should appear as a *mysterium tremendum* rather than a *mysterium fascinosum*.

The picture we have drawn of a typical conception of the Lord's Supper at the end of the nineteenth century shows great changes and developments in comparison with the position of the Reformation. It is obvious that these cannot be derived from the Reformation. They reflect the influence of entirely different factors and are connected with the movements of various kinds which have appeared during the later centuries both within and without the Lutheran communions. But the Reformation cannot be entirely absolved from blame for the one-sided and truncated conception of the sacrament that appeared in later time. The reason for this statement is twofold. In the first place, the Reformation was more intent on removing false interpretations than on presenting a positive interpretation of the sacrament. In the second place, the Reformation documents which later exercised the greatest influence gave only a partial expression to those positive ideas of the eucharist which were to be found in the writings of the Reformation. If the pregnant interpretation of the communion motif which was found in Luther's treatise of 1519, or the emphasis on the living and active Lord which is connected with the doctrine of ubiquity, had found their way into the two catechisms, these factors could have served as an effective counterbalance against the emerging individualism and against the elimination of the eucharistic element in the sacrament.

After we have drawn this picture of a celebration of the Lord's Supper in later times, we must add that great and significant changes have taken place and are taking place within the Church of Sweden as well as within other communions. If we confine ourselves to the Swedish church, it is quite evident that a turning point has been passed. We note a growing insight into the significance of the Lord's Supper and its central place in the worship life. Even if the sacramental consciousness is as yet relatively weak, it is nevertheless growing. The eucharistic liturgy has become richer. The element of praise has been strengthened. Even this indicates that a change in the conception of the Lord's Supper has taken place. The sacrament is no longer dressed in black. Eucharistic joy has found a place. Exclusive individualism gives place to a richer and fuller view of the church. We cannot here enter upon an analysis of what has happened or is happening. But it might be in place to say a few words about the various factors which have been at work. The renewal has found assistance in the Reformation through its discovery of elements which formerly were hidden. It has also found support in the new biblical orientation which we mentioned in the introduction to this book. But when we have noted these, we must realize that the most effective cause of the renewal of the sacrament lies in the Holy Communion itself, in its inseparable connection with the finished and the continuous work of Christ.

While we are concerned with the present, I call attention to a contemporary Lutheran document, the report of the Conference of the Lutheran World Federation at Lund in 1947, at which the greater part of all Lutheran communions were present. The theme of the conference was "The Lutheran Church in the World Today," and the first section dealt with the subject: "Confessing the Truth in a Confused World." This section presented a report which with a few changes was accepted by the conference as a whole. The subjects under discussion were especially the Word, the sacraments, and the church. Here we have in a certain sense a *Confessio Lutherana* from our own time. Naturally it does not have the same authoritative position as the old confessions from the days of the Reformation. But nothing corresponding to it has appeared since the sixteenth century, and it is a remarkable expression of modern Lutheranism.

In the presentation of the significance of the Lord's Supper in this document we note the following points. 1) The Lord's Supper is conceived of primarily as *communio,* fellowship with Christ. 2) The idea of the church receives strong emphasis. 3) The mystery of the real presence is maintained but freed from scholastic speculations.

The first two points—the Lord's Supper as communion with Christ and the emphasis on the church—are very closely related. "The Lord's Supper is given to us in order that by it Christ may continually nourish and build up those who are members of His Body." It "is celebrated in memory of what God did when he founded the new covenant, established through the atoning death of Christ." But it is not only a revered memory of the death of Christ. "The essential thing in the Lord's Supper is, as Luther held, that just as the eternal Word became incarnate in Christ, so He himself is present in bread and wine to build the Church which is His Body. The real presence of Christ moreover is in no way dependent on our faith, but upon the incomprehensible grace by which He wills to give himself to us in the sacrament. . . . Here the Christian enters into direct communion with his living Lord. . . . In the Lord's Supper life flows forth from Christ through His Body to all His members." [1]

The emphasis is on the active presence of Christ. The Lord's Supper is a *mysterium* which we can never fully understand. In accordance with the Lutheran tradition both transubstantiation

[1] *Proceedings of the Lutheran World Federation Assembly, Lund, Sweden, 1947* (Philadelphia, 1948), p. 16ff.

and the spiritual-symbolic interpretation are rejected. The doctrine of transubstantiation is human speculation which has nothing to do with the gospel. It is not at this point that the mystery of the gospel is found. But it is likewise a perversion when it is asserted that the bread and the wine that are blessed only signify (*significant*) the body and blood of Christ, "so that the real presence of Christ in the Lord's Supper is denied. The essence of the Lord's Supper is the real presence of Christ. As it has pleased God to speak to us by means of simple human words, so that we can say that this is in truth God's Word, without its therefore ceasing to be human words, so it has also pleased Christ really and truly to come to us by these simple means. Christ himself is present in the Bread and the Cup that we bless without their being changed into anything other than what they are. The mystery of the Lord's Supper is nothing else than the mystery of the gospel as a whole. It is the mystery of the fact that God has sent into this world of death Him who is Prince of Life and has called us to become one with Him and to receive a share in His life."

It is unnecessary to comment on this document, but we need to emphasize a few points. It is clear that the communion motif has found the same central position which it had in Luther's treatise of 1519. When the document speaks of the gift of the Lord's Supper, the forgiveness of sins is not directly mentioned, but the reality is present in a positive sense. The Christ who is present in the Lord's Supper is the living and active Lord. He has attached his presence to the bread and the wine. Communion with him involves life of his life. The interpretation of the Lord's Supper is exuberant with the joy of thanksgiving. The brief presentation is thoroughly biblical and, in regard to the conception of the church, very strongly Pauline.

Part III

The Teaching of the New Testament

11

For What Purpose?

In the previous section we considered the Lutheran Reformation and to some extent its later development. The background of our presentation was the varied estimates of the Reformation which we encounter in the modern ecumenical discussions of the Lord Supper. No ecumenical discussion can ignore the Reformation. Whatever starting-point we may take, we must sooner or later define our attitude to it and to its interpretation of the eucharist. If all ecumenical endeavor is an attempt to overcome and transcend contradictory views, the Reformation can supply all the material needed, since no movement has made such a deep and lasting impression in Christian history.

It is obvious that there will be a difference in the position taken toward the Reformation by those communions which belong to the Protestant tradition and those outside of it. A theology which belongs within the Reformation must assume a responsibility for its own inheritance and be on guard lest insights dearly won should be lost. But nevertheless such a theology cannot go to the Reformation in order to find final answers to its questions. If it should do so, it would have denied its inheritance from the start. There is nothing more evident than that the Reformation did not arrogate to itself and its confessions a final and decisive authority. On the contrary, it has always pointed to the Bible as the highest authority for what is legitimately Christian.

But fortunately it is not only the Protestant communions that refer to this highest authority. The biblical message constitutes in reality and in principle a common platform for all branches of the church which participate in the ecumenical work. The Anglican communion, which also belongs to the Protestant group, although it at the same time emphasizes its solidarity with the "catholic" tradition, testifies clearly to the Bible as the highest authority. It might seem that the Eastern Orthodox church is a little less clear on this point, insofar as it speaks of "tradition" as an authority alongside of the Bible. But since the Eastern Orthodox church does not permit tradition to present statements in conflict with the testimony of the Bible, its intention is evidently to maintain the authority of the Bible. In this connection there is no direct reason for us to discuss the complicated question of Scripture and tradition within the Roman church. But whatever theories we may have in regard to the relationship between these two factors, the interest in a biblical orientation is growing.

A review of the ecumenical discussions since 1920 reveals that we may distinguish two different periods. During the first period the discussions on Faith and Order were concerned with establishing what was held in common and what separated us. This procedure was no doubt both inevitable and useful at the beginning of the discussions. Through these confrontations we learned to know one another and to see where the real difficulties were. But negotiations of this kind in the long run prove unsatisfactory. They could not really lead to positive results. It became more and more clear that we must turn to a more serious study of the Scriptures to which all the parties appealed. This new turn appeared very clearly at the Conference on Faith and Order in Lund, 1952. It had been prepared through the vigorous biblical research which had made so many contacts across denominational lines. There can be no question but that this is the only direction in which we can advance. As we move from the Reformation back to the New

Testament, we are in perfect agreement with the tendencies within modern ecumenical discussions.

For what purpose then are we now concerned with the New Testament? We do not intend to produce any direct exegetical studies, or to define our attitude to the many exegetical problems about which scholarly opinions are divided. We do not intend, for instance, to discuss the relationship between the various narratives of the institution of the Lord's Supper, the original words which Jesus used, or on what day Jesus held this last meal with his disciples. We are not concerned with the relationship between the agape feasts and the separate celebration of the eucharist, nor will we pay any more attention than is necessary to the development of the celebration of the sacrament within the New Testament period. We shall not engage in a discussion of the many and varied ritual problems which are connected with the celebration of the eucharist in the New Testament. The latest exegetical research has produced much material of this kind and claims to have found, not only many more fragments of the worship in the ancient church than was formerly expected, but also the fundamental structure of the worship service.

All these things are tremendously interesting. They indicate that worship had a central place in the ancient church and points to the Lord's Supper as the center and climax of the original cult. But no matter how exciting it might be to participate in the research of the ritual, prayers, confessions, etc., we have no real reason in this connection to investigate these areas. It would be different if our dependence on the New Testament involved patterning our worship services as closely as possible on those of the ancient church. Luther has said at one time that our celebration of the eucharist ought to be an imitation of the Supper which the Lord held on the last evening with his disciples. This may be regarded as a random thought which had no influence on his orders of the mass, nor was it in harmony with his conception of our dependence on the Bible.

The traces of an order of service which we find in the New Testament cannot, any more than the organizational pattern, be decisive for later generations. The authority of the New Testament was not minimized when the later church added prayers and hymns which were not found in the ancient church, or when the celebration gradually assumed a much richer form. But we must demand that everything which may appear in a Christian celebration of the Lord's Supper harmonize with and stand the test of that message which the New Testament brings.

In these statements we have already indicated the purpose of this third part. We come to the New Testament with all the questions which have been raised in modern ecumenical discussions, and also with those questions from the Reformation which are still relevant. We want to confront our discoveries with the testimony of Scripture. We must first of all listen to what the New Testament as a whole has to say about the significance of the Lord's Supper. We must look at the picture of the eucharist which the various biblical authors present, especially Paul, John, and the Letter to the Hebrews. This confrontation does not mean that eucharistic ideas from later times are to be judged according to biblical formulations, as if we were concerned with paragraphs in a code of law. Biblical authority is of a different kind. It does not mean that nothing can be said in the Christian church which was not already said in its fundamental document. Such a negative statement would deny the biblical promise of the guidance of the Spirit. Rather, the truth of the matter may be stated this way: Just as the Christian message as a whole, the gospel, is given once and for all, so the character and constitution of the Lord's Supper is given once and for all. This fact imposes some very definite demands on all later interpretations of the Lord's Supper.

The main concern of this book is the status of the idea of sacrifice in the Lord's Supper. We must inquire especially, therefore, as to what the New Testament has to say on this subject. But this question cannot be isolated and treated by itself. It must be examined in connection with the New Testament conception of the Lord's Supper as a whole. In addition the Lord's Supper, too, must be seen in the total context in which it appears. If this were not done, some necessary perspective would be lost. Our first task, therefore, is to pay attention to this general context.

12

The Eucharist and the Gospel

The eucharist is inseparably connected with the redemptive act of God in Jesus Christ. This redemptive act is from one point of view a finished act, while from another point of view it is continuous. Both of these viewpoints are equally emphasized. The eucharist has its presupposition in what has been once for all accomplished, and at the same time it is the bearer of the continuous work.

The work which Christ was sent into the world to accomplish has been finished. Christ has done what God wanted him to do. The intended result has been attained and has been accepted by God. Any addition to this work is out of the question. To this the New Testament Scriptures bear unanimous testimony in the most varied ways.

The act which is finished is the act of atonement. "God was in Christ reconciling the world to himself" (II Cor. 5:19). This is something that *has* happened and has created an entirely new life situation. A new covenant has been established, "not in a written code but in the Spirit" (II Cor. 3:6); a covenant which is founded not on law but on the gospel. The words of institution of the Lord's Supper speak especially of this new covenant. A new age, the age of life, has come with liberation from slavery under the destructive powers of sin and death. Christ has "abolished death and brought life and immortality to light through the gospel" (II Tim. 1:10). In order to accomplish this work Christ had to suffer death on the cross. But now he is no longer the Suffering Servant but the living Lord whom God has exalted and given a name above every name (Phil. 2:9). The exaltation testifies that the victory has been won, and that Christ in his earthly ministry finished the work which God entrusted to him. God "raised him from the dead and made him sit at his right hand in the heavenly places, far above all rule and authority and power and dominion, and above every name that is named, not only in this age but also in that which is to come" (Eph. 1:20-21).

The finished work of Christ embraces his whole earthly life. It begins in the incarnation. Christ "did not count equality with God a thing to be grasped, but emptied himself, taking the form of a servant" (Phil. 2:6-7). It continues in obedience and service, in struggle and suffering, and it issues finally in death on the cross, the climax and the end. In all this the work of Christ appears as a sacrifice. The reality in this sacrifice is his obedience to the will of the heavenly Father and his love poured out in full solidarity with those who live in bondage under the destructive powers of sin and death. This theme recurs in constantly changing expressions in the Synoptics, John, Paul, and the other New Testament writings.

In the Synoptic Gospels the Messiah, the Son of Man, is one with his people. He represents them before God. His suffering and death makes expiation for their sins and wipes out their guilt. In the words of Anton Fridrichsen, the atonement is not a transaction between God and Christ for the benefit of humanity; it is not a triangular drama, for Jesus suffers and dies in accordance with God's will and on behalf of the people of God.[1] *Anti* means both "instead of" and "on behalf of." He liberates the people from their guilt and punishment which belong under the power of Satan. This means a radical recreation of the people in and through the

[1] Anton Fridrichsen, "Försoningen och kyrkan i Nya testamentet," in *Den nya kyrkosynen* (Lund, 1945), p. 51.

Messiah's triumph over death and the devil. The idea of vicariousness is very clear, but it has no juridical significance. It depends entirely on the axiom of the solidarity in life and death between the Son of Man and "the many." John widens the perspective. Jesus died "not for the nation only, but to gather into one the children of God who are scattered abroad" (John 11:52). After his exaltation he will draw all men to himself (John 12:32). He is the Lamb of God who takes away the sin of the world (John 1:29). In the letters of Paul the interpretation of the redemptive work of Christ centers in the substitutionary atonement. Christ has suffered the penalty for the sin of many; he has redeemed us from the curse of the law. All are included in the suffering and death of this one. "One has died for all; therefore all have died" (II Cor. 5:14). The all-pervading idea is that the sacrifice of Christ which was accomplished in death is the way through which God realizes his will of love and makes reconciliation.

But just as emphatically as the New Testament declares that the earthly ministry of Christ is definitive, it also testifies that his redemptive work still continues. The reconciliation is a fact. The sacrifice, as the Letter to the Hebrews states again and again, has been made once for all and is valid for all time. The new covenant has been established. That which has happened is the presupposition and the secure foundation of the Lord's Supper. But the redemptive work of Christ is not finished. It continues always under conditions created by the work perfected once for all. This continuous work is connected with the church which Christ builds on the basis of the atonement. The church is the result of the finished work of reconciliation. The risen and living Lord, Victor over the demonic forces, reigns in his church. The church is the people of God united with Christ, the new Israel. This ecclesia is inseparately united with Christ. Just as the church cannot exist without Christ, so neither does Christ exist without his ecclesia. The church is "his body." This Pauline formula is not peculiar to

Paul, but expresses the conception of the relationship between Christ and the church which is common to the whole New Testament. The parable of the vine and the branches expresses the same thing. The church has its life in and through Christ. To this extent Christ is one with his church, and the church one with him; this is the most fundamental thing that can be said about the church. But this "identity" between Christ and the church, his body, is derived entirely from the activity of Christ; the church is life of his life. This statement about "identity" is true as long as it is based on Christ and his work, but it becomes misleading if it is derived from the church. The church is what it is through the work of Christ, but Christ is not what he is through the church.

Thus the redemptive work of Christ continues in and through the church. In the New Testament the time of the church is the time between the resurrection of Christ and his Parousia. The church and everything that takes place in it stand under the eschatological perspective. Attention is directed toward "the age that is to come," toward the fulfilment, toward that which finally will be revealed in glory. But we would interpret this eschatological perspective in a one-sided and narrow manner if we make it refer exclusively to something that is to come. It is characteristic for the New Testament that it combines the future with the present. In reality the church in this age is already the bearer of that new age which will be revealed in glory when all is finished. The New Testament, therefore, places a very strong emphasis on the present. "Behold, now is the acceptable time; behold, now is the day of salvation" (II Cor. 6:2). Now, says the Letter to the Hebrews, we have tasted "the powers of the age to come" (Heb. 6:5).

If the work of salvation is to be brought to all the world, "to all people," the message of Christ must be proclaimed. When Paul tells us that God has in Christ reconciled the world to himself, he adds immediately: "God was in Christ . . . entrusting to us the message of reconciliation. So we are ambassadors for Christ" (II

Cor. 5:19-20). Preaching, the proclamation, is the necessary condition for the upbuilding of the church of Christ. "And how are they to believe in him of whom they have never heard? And how are they to hear without a preacher?" (Rom. 10:14). The preaching of the gospel draws men to Christ. But this does not imply a setting aside of baptism and the Lord's Supper. The incorporation into that ecclesia which is the body of Christ takes place in the sacraments. That time is past when it could be maintained that the church and the sacraments had only a secondary place in the New Testament. Participation in salvation involves becoming a member in the body of Christ, and this incorporation into his body, this fellowship, this *koinonia*, occurs through the sacraments.

Baptism is the initiatory act through which a person becomes a member in the ecclesia and participates in the rights and privileges of adoption. He obtains fellowship with Christ in his death and life. "If we have been united with him in a death like his, we shall certainly be united with him in a resurrection like his" (Rom. 6:5). But, as these words have already indicated, baptism is more than an act of initiation. It embraces the whole Christian life. It involves a dying to the power of sin and death. This dying is not a single act; it is something that continually takes place in a constant struggle with the demonic forces.

The *koinonia* with Christ which is established in baptism is renewed, maintained, nourished, and strengthened through the Lord's Supper. Here the Lord continually re-establishes the fellowship of the new covenant with his church and its members. The Lord's Supper is the bond of union in the church's *koinonia* with Christ, and therefore also the center and climax in the worship of the church. Thus the Lord's Supper builds the church of Christ on earth. The Lord continues his redemptive work in the church. Here, as the Letter to the Hebrews says, "the powers of the age to come" are at work right in the present.

This review of the context in which the Lord's Supper stands has shown us several points: (1) The foundation of the Lord's Supper is the act of reconciliation accomplished once for all. (2) The Lord's Supper is an instrument used by the living Lord in his continuous, redemptive work in the church. (3) The Lord's Supper is, therefore, inseparably connected with the conception of the church that we find in the New Testament.

13

The Crucified and the Living One

If we trace the history of the eucharist through the centuries, we encounter a number of varied interpretations of the sacrament. This is a perfectly natural development. But at times the word "development" is too weak. The differences may be so great and profound that they lead to sharp antitheses. In fact some of the most bitter doctrinal conflicts in Christianity have been concerned with that sacrament which is inseparately connected with the Lord's prayer "that they may all be one" (John 17:21), and which is therefore the sacrament of Christian unity. There have been many reasons for the conflicts about the Lord's Supper. We shall not make an attempt to enumerate them. In this connection we wish to call attention to just one very essential reason for differences and conflicts, which is present even within the New Testament. The interpretation of the sacrament has been exclusively associated either with the death of Christ on the cross or with the risen and living Lord. The second of these is to be found in the earlier church history, the first has appeared in various forms during later periods. I can refer for examples to the later Middle Ages and to the description of the situation during the nineteenth century in the previous section.

In 1946 there appeared an article on the celebration of the eucharist in the New Testament by Eduard Schweizer. I mention it especially because of the title: "Das Abendmahl, eine Vergegen-

wärtigung des Todes Jesu oder ein eschatologisches Freudenmahl?" [1]
The question posed by the author is concerned with the alternative:
either a one-sided connection with the death of Jesus, or an
equally one-sided connection with the risen and living Lord. The
starting point of the article is the discussion which New Testament exegetes have held in recent decades about various interpretations of the Lord's Supper within the New Testament. These
discussions arose especially on the basis of the book by H. Lietzmann, *Messe und Herrenmahl* (1926), in which he pointed out
a sharp difference between a Jerusalem and a Pauline type of the
sacrament. By way of introduction Schweizer underscores the great
significance which this question must have "for the whole life of
the Christian congregation." He is right, of course, for the acceptance of one alternative and the rejection of the other would
certainly have very serious consequences. Schweizer, however,
wants to show in his article that there is no compelling reason to
play up one alternative against the other. He is in agreement with
what leading exegetes held even at the time when the article was
written, and which was later fully accepted. We shall, however,
leave the question of the relationship between the celebration of
the sacrament in Acts and the Pauline "type," and instead turn
our attention to a difference in the interpretation of the Lord's
Supper which actually is found in the New Testament. This difference is documented in Paul's First Letter to the Corinthians and
may be regarded as the first eucharistic conflict in the history of
Christianity.

Paul had found that many abuses and serious offenses occurred
in Corinth in connection with the celebration of the Supper. It
was clear to him that this unworthy conduct was connected with a
false and perverted view of the significance of the Lord's Supper.
In his fight against abuses the Apostle relates what happened at

[1] Eduard Schweizer, "Das Abendmahl, eine Vergegenwaertigung des Todes
Jesu oder ein eschatologisches Freudenmahl?" in *Theologisches Zeitschrift*
(Basel, 1946), p. 81ff.

Jesus' last meal with his disciples, and then he adds: "As often as you eat this bread and drink the cup, you proclaim the Lord's death until he comes." He evidently wants to tell the Corinthians that the celebration of the Lord's Supper in the Christian church is inseparably connected with that which happened in the circle of the disciples in the night in which the Lord was betrayed, and that the eucharist continually contemporizes the death of Christ: it involves a "proclamation" of Jesus' death. Now we may ask: What was the reason that Paul in his struggle with the false teachers emphasized just these points of view? What was the content of the misinterpretation which led to such dire consequences?

These questions have recently been subjected to a penetrating study by Bo Reicke in a book entitled *Diakonie, Festfreude und Zelos in Verbindung mit der altchristlischen Agapefeier.*

Reicke maintains that the false teachers toward whom Paul directs his criticism were docetic Gnostics, libertines, and at the same time Judaizers. "The Christ party" in Corinth were concerned exclusively with the exalted, heavenly Christ and with the fulness of the spirit of those who were connected with him in a true gnosis.[2] They acted as if the Parousia and the fulfilment had already taken place. The death of Jesus and his earthly ministry as a whole had been set aside. The eucharistic celebration was characterized by spiritual enthusiasm. The Lord's Supper was transformed into a festival of triumph. Love was shunted aside and egoistical joy took over completely. This pseudo-sacramental hedonism is, according to Reicke, a logical result of Docetism. "When the sacramental elements lose their connection with the death of Christ, there appears a one-sided emphasis on the connection with the exalted Lord and the heavenly life. With frenzied desire and egoistical enthusiasm they consume the elements as a kind of heavenly food."[3]

[2] Bo Reicke, *Diakonie, Festfreude und Zelos in Verbindung mit der altchristlischen Agapefeier* (Uppsala, 1951), p. 279.
[3] *Ibid.*, p. 281.

Paul finds it necessary to remind these docetic fanatics about some very serious facts: that Jesus died and was buried (I Cor. 15:3ff), and what happened on that last evening. By thus quoting the words of institution, he attacks the celebration of the eucharist in Corinth, and he emphasizes his point by adding: "For as often as you eat this bread and drink the cup, you proclaim the Lord's death until he comes."

Paul is therefore attacking a docetic Gnosticism. But this has at the same time a Judaizing character. Reicke points out that a docetic Christology agrees well with a Judaizing tendency and admirably serves its purpose. (1) If his death was of no great consequence, the guilt of the Jews becomes less serious. (2) The prevalent Jewish doctrine of God with its strict transcendentalism could remain unchanged if the incarnation, the life and death of Jesus, were minimized. (3) The conception of the Messiah in the apocalyptic tradition could be retained if they did not refer too much to the suffering Jesus.[4]

In what relationship does this Corinthian caricature of the Lord's Supper stand to the celebration in the ancient church as related in Acts? Reicke points out that in Jerusalem after the outpouring of the Spirit they lived in "an ecstatic festival spirit," and that they celebrated the common, cultic meal with joy. He deems it therefore quite natural that there was a connection between Jerusalem and Corinth. But at the same time he points out that "the festival joy" in Corinth became corrupted partly because a pretentious gnosis had taken the place of that "singleness of heart" of which Acts speaks, and partly because in their selfish indulgence they had forgotten the mutual service of love. In this controversy between Paul and the Corinthians Paul maintained "a retrospective, serious, ethical, and corporate conception, but the Corinthians held to a lustful [begierig], eschatological, joyous, licentious, material and selfish practice."[5]

---

[4] *Ibid.*, p. 282.   [5] *Ibid.*, p. 290ff.

As we look at this interpretation of the first controversy in regard to the Lord's Supper, the Corinthian celebration appears as a caricature of the celebration in the ancient Jerusalem church. The appearance of this caricature, however, indicates what a large place eucharistic joy had in the celebration of the sacrament in the ancient church. This fact is corroborated by Reicke's careful analysis of the joyous character of the Old Testament festivals as a background of the ancient celebration of the sacrament. This heritage has contributed effectively to the development of the ancient Christian cult. It is true, of course, that the main reason for eucharistic joy is the resurrection and the cultic presence of the risen Lord; but if we regard this as the only cause, we build on too narrow a foundation. The forms of the ancient Christian cult are related to the festival ideologies in the Old Testament. "The resurrection of Christ is undeniably the *causa efficiens* of eucharistic joy, but the Old Testament festival ideologies are the *causa substantialis.*" [6]

That there existed a deep-seated and fundamental opposition between Paul and the false teachers in Corinth is, as we have seen, undeniable. It manifested itself not only in matters of practice but also in the conceptions which underlay them. Here it was a matter of the utmost significance that the cultic festival lacked any connection with the death of Jesus—or for that matter with his earthly life at all. If we now turn to Paul's statement about the Lord's Supper in the Corinthian letters and the narratives in Acts that deal with the ancient Christian celebration, we clearly find differences in emphases and viewpoints. But scholars have become less and less inclined to follow Lietzmann in his attempt to establish a fundamental conflict between a Pauline-Hellenistic and a Jerusalem-Judaistic interpretation of the Lord's Supper.

Such a fundamental conflict would undeniably have existed if the Jerusalem church had emphasized the resurrection to the ex-

[6] *Ibid.,* p. 226.

clusion of the death on the cross, and Paul had emphasized the death of Jesus to the exclusion of the resurrection. The fact, of course, is that the accounts of the cultic celebration in Acts do not *directly* refer to the death of Jesus. But the question is what conclusions we can draw from this fact.

It is clear that the cult meals in the ancient church are closely connected with and a continuation of the meals which Jesus shared with his disciples. In his book, *The Celebration of the Eucharist in the Ancient Church,* Nils Johansson emphasizes that the Last Supper must not be isolated, but must be seen in the context of the earlier, messianic meals during Jesus' ministry. This is also true of the ancient Christian cultic meals. "The table fellowship in the kingdom of God, which began while the hidden Son of Man was here on earth, had to be continued during the interval between his resurrection and Parousia. It occupied the same place as during Jesus' earthly life." [7] Oscar Cullmann finds the most immediate background for the early Christian agape-eucharist in the meals which the risen Lord shared with his disciples. He maintains that the ancient church in its eucharistic meals looks back to those Easter meals which according to the Gospel of Luke began already on the first Easter Day: the meal which the disciples on the way to Emmaus shared with the One who made himself known "in the breaking of bread," and the meal together with the eleven on the same day. He finds a connection between these Easter meals and the ancient eucharist in the speech in which Peter says that God raised Christ "and made him manifest; not to all the people but to us who were chosen by God as witnesses, who ate and drank with him after he rose from the dead" (Acts 10:41).[8]

But neither one of these scholars would hold that the eucharistic meal in the ancient church had no connection with the last supper

[7] Nils Johansson, *Det urkristna nattvardsfirandet (The Celebration of the Lord's Supper in the Ancient Church)* (Lund, 1944), p. 271.
[8] Oscar Cullmann, *Early Christian Worship,* tr. by A. S. Todd and J. B. Torrance (Chicago: 1956), p. 15.

and with the death of Christ. Cullmann, to be sure, speaks of two "types of eucharists," but even though he emphasizes the immediate connection between the ancient eucharist and the meals of the risen Lord with his disciples after Easter, he also maintains that Jesus' last supper with his disciples is the common origin of both the ancient and the Pauline "types," and the eschatological viewpoint is common to both.[9] Johansson sums up his view of the matter in the following statement. "The vicarious suffering and death of the Son of Man were just as much as his resurrection the reason for his expected and imminent return. His suffering and death were an integral part of that redemptive act of God which belonged to the last time and constituted the foundation of the mood of exultation." Johansson also reckons with the possibility that the unusual expression, "the breaking of bread" as a designation of the meal, was due to the fact that "the bread through this act was changed into a symbol of the body of Jesus broken in death." [10]

In *Theologische Literaturzeitung* (1954), Eduard Schweizer has published an article under the title: "Das Herrenmahl im Neuen Testament, ein Forschungsbericht" [11] ("The Lord's Supper in the New Testament: a Report on Research"). In his analysis of relevant literature he points out among other things that Paul in his quotation of the words of institution refers to what he "had received from the Lord." However these words may be interpreted, "it is clear that Paul knows of no different or earlier tradition. When we realize that he lived with people from Jerusalem for several years (Barnabas, Mark, Silas); that three years after his conversion he had been in Jerusalem at least fourteen days (Gal. 1:8); and that he must have participated in the celebration of the Lord's Supper in various congregations, it is difficult to believe that Paul would have formulated his statement as he does if he had

---

[9] *Ibid.,* p. 16.
[10] Johansson, *op. cit.,* p. 270.
[11] Eduard Schweizer, "Das Herrenmahl im Neuen Testament, ein Forschungsbericht," *Theologische Literaturzeitung* (1954), 577ff.

found anywhere a eucharist which had reference only to the eschatological fulfilment and not to the death, or to the body and blood of Christ. In addition the idea of the covenant implies a knowledge of its origin in the blood of the covenant and its fulfilment in the kingdom of God." [12] We find the same important point of view in the book by A. J. B. Higgins, *The Lord's Supper in the New Testament:* "Paul was not the originator of the type of Eucharist which was predominantly a feast in memory of Christ's death, because the first 'Do this in remembrance of me' belonged to a tradition he had received." [13]

Finally in this connection I quote a carefully balanced statement by H. Riesenfeld. "It is entirely probable that the members of the primitive church knew from the beginning that Jesus had 'instituted' the Lord's Supper by his command to repeat what had happened at the last supper. Even if the words, 'do this in remembrance of me,' do not occur in all the traditions of the words of institution, their appearance in a definite form indicates that at an early date the Christian church was conscious of Jesus' will that the congregation come together for the breaking of bread. Consequently it is not correct to see a continuation from the meals during Jesus' earthly ministry to the church's cultic breaking of bread, bypassing the last meal 'in the night in which he was betrayed.' On the contrary, the institution of the eucharist is the lens which gathers up all the ideas of former table fellowship from the time that Jesus taught and worked in the regions of Palestine, and transmits them to the following ages in the situation of the church." Riesenfeld thinks it is very probable that Paul, "the great thinker of the ancient church, theologically clarified the connection between the eucharist and the atoning death of Christ, just as he did with the sacrament of baptism. But a presupposition for this theology, not a result of it, is that the line of connection between

[12] *Ibid.,* p. 587ff.
[13] A. J. B. Higgins, *The Lord's Supper in the New Testament* (Chicago: Regnery, 1952), p. 59.

the Last Supper and the cultic fellowship of the congregation has appeared as something obviously given." [14]

We would engage in a meaningless and impossible task if we were to bring the primitive church and Paul into uniformity, or if we should assume that there was one strict and well-defined doctrine of the Lord's Supper in the New Testament. Already within the New Testament we find a number of "eucharistic motifs," and it is obvious that different emphases result in different forms or types.

It is clear that the resurrection constitutes the immediate background of eucharistic meals in the primitive church. It is very likely that Cullmann is right when he so emphatically points to the Lord's table fellowship with his disciples after the resurrection. What happens is that the resurrection so to speak produces (releases) the eucharistic meals. This is in reality quite obvious, for without the resurrection there would have been no church and no eucharist. But if we should hold, on the basis that Acts does not directly mention the death on the cross in connection with the eucharistic meals, that therefore the cultic meal had become separated from Jesus' suffering and death, we would be guilty of drawing a very rash conclusion. The apostles who constituted the original nucleus and who exercised the leadership in the primitive church had followed the Master during his earthly ministry and had sat at the table with him at the last supper. A "docetic" conception would have been impossible for them. The Docetism of the false teachers in Corinth reveals the fundamental difference in the celebration of the eucharist between the primitive church and the people whom Paul opposed in Corinth. Whatever connection there might have been between individual members of the congregation in Jerusalem and the Corinthians, it is clear that the Corinthian feast of joy is a coarse caricature of the eucharistic

[14] H. Riesenfeld, "Nattvarden i Nya testamentet" ("The Lord's Supper in the New Testament"), in *Jesus Kristus er tilstede*, 1952, p. 18. Hereafter cited as "Nattvarden."

table fellowship in Acts. But there is no essential opposition between Paul and the primitive church.

Such an opposition would be present if the Lord's Supper stood in an exclusive relationship either to the living Lord or to the death of Jesus on the cross. But just as Jesus' earthly life and his death on the cross could not have disappeared from the consciousness of the primitive church, so the Lord's Supper for Paul is not simply a sad commemoration of the death of Jesus. Such an interpretation does not fit into the theology of Paul. It is true that he tells the Corinthians that while he is among them he has determined "to know nothing among you except Jesus Christ and him crucified" (I Cor. 2:2). But we read also in the same letter: "If Christ has not been raised, then our preaching is in vain and your faith is in vain" (I Cor. 15:14). This statement reveals how Paul ties together death and resurrection in an inseparable unity, and how he discovers the significance of the redemptive act in this context. Death would not have been the act of redemption if it had not been followed by the resurrection.

The contrast between Paul and the false teachers in Corinth was not that they spoke only of the living Lord and Paul only about death. What Paul wants to tell them is that that the risen Lord is no one else than he who suffered death on the cross. He is therefore anxious to impress upon them the connection between the Lord's Supper and death. The last supper points to death and furnishes an interpretation of death as an act of redemption. Every celebration of the sacrament in the church of Christ must therefore be a proclamation of that redemptive act which is comprised in his death. If the Lord's Supper lost its connection with this redemptive act of death, it would lose its essential content. The remembrance, anamnesis, of which the apostle speaks is not only a reminder of what once happened, a recollection of the suffering and death of the Savior, but also an actualizing of his redemptive act. It becomes, to quote N. A. Dahl, *une réalité présente* (a present reality): that which once happened moves as it were into the present and becomes a living and contemporaneous reality.[15]

Closely connected with this view of anamnesis is the idea Paul expresses in I Corinthians 10:16: "The cup of blessing which we bless, is it not a participation in the blood of Christ? The bread which we break, is it not a participation in the body of Christ?" This *koinonia* with the body of Christ is at the same time a *koinonia* with the risen Lord.[16] In I Corinthians 10-12, Paul refers again and again to "the body of Christ." It occurs in various connections. "The associations from the idea of *soma*," says H. Riesenfeld, "extend in various directions: to the earthly Jesus who instituted the Lord's Supper, to the exalted Christ of whose body the bread is a participation, to the redemptive act of Christ which consisted in the giving of his body, and finally to the whole Christian community and its life in Christ." [17] In this connection we must observe two very important factors. In the first place, the church is the body of the risen and glorified Lord, and to participate in it involves above all a fellowship with him. In the second place, the church as the body of Christ is one body: "Because there is one loaf, we who are many are one body, for we all partake of the same loaf" (I Cor. 10:17). The dissension which is present in Corinth and which the apostle attacks is therefore an offense against the unity of the church which the Lord's Supper not only illustrates but also creates.

What we have just said indicates clearly that Paul does not relate the Lord's Supper only to the death of Jesus, and that his intention is not to interpret the sacrament as a sorrowful remembrance of his death. What he attacks in reference to the false teachers is not the Lord's Supper as a eucharistic festival of joy, but

[15] N. A. Dahl, "Anamnesis, Mémoire et commémoration dans le christianisme primitif," *Studia Theologica,* I (1947), 82ff.

[16] Cullmann, *op. cit.,* p. 98.

[17] H. Riesenfeld, "Kristen gudstjänst i ljuset av Nya testamentet," in *Svensk exegetisk arsbok* (1951), p. 55. Hereafter cited as "Kristen gudstjänst."

rather that caricature of joy which characterized their celebration. Paul speaks frequently in his letters about joy. "We work with you for your joy" (II Cor. 1:24); "the fruit of the Spirit is . . . joy" (Gal. 5:22); and he admonishes the Philippians to rejoice in the Lord, "again I will say, Rejoice" (Phil. 4:4). It would be strange indeed if Paul should have desired to banish joy from the celebration of the Lord's Supper. In view of the unsatisfactory state of things in Corinth he wanted to point out the perils of an unworthy celebration of the sacrament, and also emphasize the obligations of mutual fellowship which are inseparably connected with the Lord's Supper. But he did not intend to banish joy from the great festival of Christian worship. Where should there be joy if not in this sacrament?

If we place in opposition the primitive Christian eucharistic joy and a Pauline sorrowful celebration of the Lord's Supper, such an interpretation of Paul would rest on assumptions which belong to a later time, but which are found neither in Paul nor in the rest of the New Testament. It is true, as we have seen, that in later times the eucharist has been associated one-sidedly with the death of Christ, and also that the celebration has been conducted in a minor key. But such an interpretation of the eucharist was impossible for Paul because the death on the cross was for him the great act of redemption which fills the heart with a deep joy of thanksgiving. Furthermore, he always conceives of death in the light of the resurrection. The cross and the resurrection constitute for Paul as for the whole New Testament an indivisible unity.

In view of what has sometimes happened in later Christian history we may add a few words about the importance of such a unified viewpoint. If we emphasize the resurrection at the expense of the cross, we reveal that we have lost sight of the price paid for the victory. Such a position indicates that we underestimate man's need and the strength of the powers of destruction. We have then also lost sight of the bitter necessity of sacrifice and death, of the bitter struggle of divine, reconciling love. The word of the resurrection is deprived of its context, it loses both its foundation and its meaning. But a one-sided emphasis on the cross with a minimizing of the resurrection also draws with it various perils. One peril is that the cross becomes simply a martyr cross and that the sufferings of Christ become sentimentalized. In this case man's attitude to the cross then becomes compassion, or an attempt at imitation. Another peril is that the cross of Christ is interpreted as a legalistic transaction between God and Christ, and that man's attitude to the atonement is reduced to an assent to what has once happened (*cum assensione cogitare*).

14

The Sacrifice

Does the Lord's Supper in the New Testament have any connection with the idea of sacrifice? We need hardly ask this question. It is obvious that it must be answered in the affirmative. The event which the narratives of the institution of the Supper describe and the interpretive words they record are sufficient evidence. The words "given for you," "shed for you," interpret both the event at the table and the act of sacrifice in death. The sacrifice is an inseparable and integral part of the Lord's Supper.

But this connection does not rest simply on the words of institution. Sacrifice has a large place in all the New Testament writings, and we meet the idea in various forms. I quote just a few statements from various books. "For the Son of man also came not to be served but to serve, and to give his life as a ransom for many" (Mark 10:45). Jesus is "the Lamb of God" (John 1:36), "the Lamb who was slain" (Rev. 5:12). "You were ransomed . . . with the precious blood of Christ, like that of a lamb without blemish or spot" (I Pet. 1:18, 19). "And for their sake I consecrate myself, that they also may be consecrated in truth" (John 17:19). Christ died "for us" (Rom. 5:8), "for all" (II Cor. 5:14). In John 11:52 we read that Jesus was to die "not for the nation only, but to gather into one the children of God who are scattered abroad." Paul writes: "Christ redeemed us from the curse of the law, having become a curse for us" (Gal. 3:13). God "sent his

Son to be the expiation for our sins" (I John 4:10). And finally, the Letter to the Hebrews is filled with meditations on sacrifice.

It is unnecessary to cite any more passages from the New Testament. But in a preliminary way we must say something about the significance of sacrifice and its biblical context. Christ's act of sacrifice was made "in our behalf" and "for all." But "in our behalf" and "for our sake" becomes also "in our stead." Christ has "been offered once to bear the sins of many" (Heb. 9:28). His suffering and sacrifice is a vicarious suffering. He is the representative of those whose burden he bears and in whose stead he offers himself. This point of view is to be found already in what the New Testament says about Jesus as the Messiah and the Son of man. In his office as Messiah he has come to establish a "new Israel," a people of God, on whom he bestows the kingdom of God, the new life in the new age and the glory of the age to come. His whole ministry serves this purpose, but the way in which the goal is finally reached goes through the sacrifice of death. This sacrifice atones for sin and guilt and redeems men from slavery under the tyrannical, demonic powers. In this way the covenant, of which the interpretive words in the Lord's Supper speak, is established.

But even if there is no doubt that there is a close relationship between the eucharist and the idea of sacrifice in the New Testament, this does not mean that we have solved the problem of this relationship. As we consider the history of the eucharist and the present ecumenical debate, two very important problems demand our attention. One deals with the relationship of God to the sacrifice of Christ, the other concerns the extent of this sacrifice.

In order to see what the Bible teaches about God's relationship to the sacrifice of Christ, it is necessary to consider the larger context in which this sacrifice occurs. However essential and dominant the idea of sacrifice may be in the Old and the New Testaments, we must point out that there is another, wider perspective which the Bible as a whole presents. The Bible perceives existence in the form of a tremendous drama; its message revolves around that struggle, *mirabile duellum,* in which God is engaged against all opposition, against hostile powers, and against everything that would enslave humanity. This conflict meets us already on the first page of the Bible, and witness to it continues until the last pages of the Book of Revelation. This fundamental perspective reveals the unity and continuity which, in spite of all diversity and dissimilarity, characterizes the biblical message. It is most important here to note that in all these events God is the active, living, and dynamic God. The God of creation is also the God of redemption, and his redemptive work begins on the morning of creation. It did not first begin when he sent his Son into the world. In this sense the New Testament is not a new beginning but rather a continuation. But it is true that the conflict now enters a decisive stage, the hour of victory. The death and resurrection of Christ signify the decisive victory over the hostile powers. He establishes the new covenant, the covenant of reconciliation. In this covenant sin and death no longer rule, but give place to righteousness and life. Slavery under the principalities and powers of the world has been abolished. He who is incorporated into the new life in the new age is "a new creation" (II Cor. 5:17), he has "passed from death to life" (John 5:24). Christ has "abolished death and brought life and immortality to light through the gospel" (II Tim. 1:10).

It would take too long to demonstrate in detail how completely this sense of victory dominates the gospel which the New Testament proclaims. In reality the gospel is identical with the victory of Christ. A few references may suffice. In his struggle with demonic powers Christ is "the stronger" (Luke 11:21ff). He has come to bring "release to the captives" (Luke 4:18). Everything has been subjected to the Son (I Cor. 15:28). "At the name of Jesus every knee should bow" (Phil. 2:10). "Now shall the ruler of this world be cast out" (John 12:31); "the ruler of this world is judged" (John 16:11). The way to death is the way to "exaltation." "The reason the Son of God appeared was to destroy the works of the devil" (I John 3:8). "That through death he might destroy him who has the power of death, that is, the devil" (Heb. 2:14). "Lo, the Lion of the tribe of Judah, the Root of David, has conquered" (Rev. 5:5).

Since the New Testament conceives of the redemptive work of Christ both from the point of view of conflict and victory, and from that of sacrifice, it might seem proper to associate God's activity with Christ's conflict and victory, but in the case of his sacrifice to conceive of God as only passive and receptive. We could justify this interpretation by pointing out that the dramatic perspective always emphasizes God's activity, and Christ in his conflict appears therefore as God's warrior. We could also point out that the sacrificing Christ bears the burden of humanity, accomplishes his sacrifice in solidarity with humanity, and consequently is humanity's representative before God. When we look closer, however, it becomes apparent that such an interpretation separates the perspective of conflict and victory from that of sacrifice in a way which is foreign to the New Testament. This is apparent for the simple reason that Christ won his victory by giving himself as a sacrifice in death. The New Testament indeed conceives of Christ in his redemptive work as the representative of both God and humanity, but not in the sense that in his victory he represents only God and in his sacrifice only humanity. It is rather that both in his victorious conflict and in his sacrifice he acts on behalf of God and on behalf of humanity.

Let us now consider these two points of view in regard to the sacrifice of Christ. This sacrifice is from one point of view a sacrifice on behalf of humanity. Christ assumes fully the conditions of humanity, i.e., the condition of sin and death. This is involved in his becoming man, in the incarnation. "The Word became flesh and dwelt among us" (John 1:14). In full solidarity with us Christ assumes the burden of our sin and guilt, and also God's wrath against sin. He was, as Paul says, "born under the law, to redeem those who were under the law" (Gal. 4:4) and under its judgment. Thus Christ's act of sacrifice, perfected once for all in his death, is vicarious and sufficient. It is an act of sacrifice made in obedience to the will of the heavenly Father, and thus a sacrifice offered to and received by God.

But this conception of the sacrifice of Christ would be a caricature of what the New Testament teaches if we isolate it and think of God as the one who simply accepts the sacrifice Christ brings on behalf of humanity. No, the New Testament tells us clearly that God actively participates in what happens and that he himself brings the offering. This activity of God is revealed in the fact that God sent his Son into the world. When the Gospel of John says that "God gave his only Son" (3:16), it implies that this sending was God's own sacrifice.

But God's activity is not limited to this initiatory act. Christ pursued his way of sacrifice unto death in obedience to the will of God. It was God's will that suffering and death should strike him. He not only offered himself; God gave him as a sacrifice. God "gave" him not only by sending him into the world but also by sending him to death. From one point of view his suffering and death were a result of the attack by the hostile powers on him. But from a more serious point of view this was a case of divine necessity. It was God's will that this evil should strike him. His enemies did not offer him; they only did violence to him. We would not express the whole truth if we said that God simply "permitted" him to be put to death. He gave himself, and God gave him as a sacrifice.

Even so we have not yet arrived at the most profound conception of God's activity. If we say simply that God's relationship to the sacrifice of Christ consisted in his sending the Son into the world and later permitting him to go the way of sacrifice to death, this might be interpreted to mean that God stood at a distance as a spectator of the act which Christ performed. But in that way we would not express the view of the New Testament. It is obvious that the New Testament regards Christ's redemptive act as God's own work. This view has been given a classic expression in the words of Paul: "All this is from God, who through Christ reconciled us to himself and gave us the ministry of reconciliation; that is, God was in Christ reconciling the world to himself" (II Cor. 5:18-19). God himself is active in the redemptive work of Christ. The love we have learned to know because "he laid down his life for us" (I John 3:16) is God's own love.

We have previously seen that Christ's vicarious solidarity with humanity is connected with his incarnation. But now we find how his incarnation unites the work of God and of Christ. It was God who in Christ reconciled the world to himself. The atonement of Christ is altogether a work of God's own love. If we deny this, we must at the same time deny the reality of the incarnation. What happens in and with the sacrifice of Christ is that the love of God breaks through all hindrances and even through the divine judgment that rests upon sinful humanity. "The Father who dwells in me does his works" (John 14:10).[1]

This biblical view of sacrifice overturns common conceptions of sacrifice in religion. In the world's religions there is an abundance of sacrificial fires. By these offerings men have sought to propitiate God and obtain his favor. But in the sacrifice of Christ everything is different. Here God's own love goes the way of sacrifice, assumes the burden of the world's woe, enters into suffering and death, and by so doing wins the victory which establishes the new covenant, parts the veil asunder and provides an access to the Holy of Holies.

[1] Cf. Charles H. Dodd, *The Interpretation of the Fourth Gospel* (London: Cambridge Univ. Pr., 1953), p. 256ff.

This view does not mean that we eliminate what we have said before, that Christ acts on behalf of humanity, and that God accepts his sacrifice. The resurrection and the exaltation testify of this "acceptance." If in this connection we use the traditional word of theology, which is also biblical, Christ's "satisfaction," it would mean not only that Christ through his obedience in death has "satisfied" the God who in his love radically condemns everything that is evil, but also and above all that he has "satisfied" God's love and made satisfaction for the God who himself is love.

The term merit (*meritum*) which a later theology used in speaking of the sacrifice of Christ is similar to the term satisfaction. Neither of these words occur in the New Testament, but both may be regarded as biblical if properly interpreted. The "merit" of Christ consists in that in obedience to his heavenly Father he accomplished the work he was sent into the world to do. It is, therefore, on the "merit" of this act that the new covenant could be established, a new age could appear, and a new relationship between God and the world could be constituted. In this sense the sacrifice of Christ, the sacrifice of reconciliation, has a "meritorious" character. In the sight of God it is eminently meritorious. Christ is "that living stone, rejected by men but in God's sight chosen and precious" (I Pet. 2:4). But this does not mean that God is merely the receiver, and that the sacrifice of Christ should be regarded as "a compensation" given to God. The merit is rather that this sacrifice was the way through which it became possible for God, or through which God made it possible, to create the new situation under the new covenant. It may thus be said that God became reconciled to the world, but only if we incorporate this statement into the context which is of greatest importance in the Bible: God was in Christ reconciling the world to himself.

We have discussed rather fully the relationship of God to the sacrifice of Christ. In this presentation we have not referred directly to any New Testament eucharistic passages, but have tried to indicate the background against which the sacrificial motif in the Lord's Supper appears. For anyone who knows something of the later history of the Lord's Supper it will be obvious that the attitude theology has taken to this fundamental problem—God's relationship to the sacrifice of Christ and the atonement—has markedly influenced the interpretation of the eucharist. The greatest peril has been that the biblical view of God's activity has been more or less suppressed. The result of this we will have opportunity to examine later.

We now go on to the second of the two problems: the extent of the sacrifice of Christ. The questions we have reference to here we have encountered frequently in ecumenical discussions. We recall that Hicks in his memorial presented to the Edinburgh Conference points out how the Middle Ages restricted the sacrifice to "death and the immolation." We recall also how the reaction to this one-sided emphasis was expressed in the statement by the conference: "If sacrifice is understood as it was by our Lord and his followers and in the early church, it includes, not His death only, but the obedience of his earthly ministry, and his risen and ascended life, in which He still does His Father's will and ever liveth to make intercession for us."

When we ask how the New Testament conceives of the extent of the sacrifice of Christ, we find that this is a complex subject in which two questions especially claim our attention. First, does the New Testament regard the period before his death as a part of his sacrifice? Second, is it biblically correct to speak of a sacrifice performed by the heavenly Christ? If we may do so, what significance does this "sacrifice" have, and how is it related to the sacrifice on the cross?

There is no doubt but that the New Testament obviously connects sacrifice with the death on the cross. But it is just as evident that it does not isolate death and relate sacrifice to it alone. His death is a part of a larger context; it is the climax and the conclusion of his total service. Christ did not come into the world only to die; he went the way of death because only in this way could he accomplish the mission he had been sent to perform. From one point of view all his work is a continuous offering, completed and perfected in the sacrifice of death. His obedience, says Paul, was not only an obedience in death but *unto* death; "he humbled himself and became obedient unto death" (Phil. 2:8). The good shepherd gives his life for the sheep (John 10:11, 15), but this is not the only act of sacrifice. It is the supreme manifestation of self-sacrificing love. "Greater love has no man than this, that a man lay down his life for his friends" (John 15:13). John regards death as "a supreme act of self-sacrifice." [2] But it is at the same time the possibility of a new age. "Unless a grain of wheat falls into the earth and dies, it remains alone; but if it dies, it bears much fruit" (John 12:24).

If we want to see, however, how the whole earthly life of Jesus is connected with the sacrifice, we cannot simply consider individual passages in which this motif appears more or less clearly. It is more important to notice the part which the Suffering Servant of the Lord (Isa. 53) plays in relation to the biblical conception of Jesus as the Messiah and to his mission as a whole. It is against the background of the Suffering Servant that we must understand the gospel narratives—how Jesus from the time of the temptation in the wilderness had to contend against false conceptions of the Messiah. It is certain that Jesus conceived of his mission from this point of view. The theme of the Suffering Servant provides a broad foundation for the idea of sacrifice and permits it to appear almost everywhere in the biblical testimony of Christ. I quote here a few words by Anders Nygren on this subject. "If we have glimpsed the strange figure of the *Ebed-Jahve* and of its even stranger realization in Jesus Christ, if we have sharpened our perception of the theme by reference to the Servant-Songs, then we will encounter this

[2] *Ibid.,* p. 249.

theme nearly every step of the way through the New Testament. The impression cannot be avoided that Jesus lived entirely in the *Ebed-Jahve* sphere. There he found the confirmation for the mission on which he knew that he had been sent. There existed the basic features of his new messianic concept in which the Messiah-Christ was no longer an earthly ruler, but one who, in representative suffering, took upon himself the sin of the world and who gave himself a ransom for many. The concept of Christ the King finds its interpretation in the crucified Redeemer." [3]

The New Testament connects the idea of sacrifice with the whole earthly life of Jesus. It goes even farther: the sacrifice begins in the incarnation. When Paul, having the Suffering Servant in mind, speaks about Christ's form of a servant, this title appears in a larger context. "Though he was in the form of God, [he] did not count equality with God a thing to be grasped, but emptied himself, taking the form of a servant, being born in the likeness of men" (Phil. 2:6-7). As we have seen already, the incarnation is an act of sacrifice by God. But it is at the same time an act of sacrifice by the "pre-existent" Son. If for Paul the incarnation is the starting point of the redemptive work of Christ in his character as Servant, this is true to an even greater extent of John. It is characteristic of him that he places his interpretation of the Lord's Supper in chapter six, to which we will return shortly, in the immediate context of the incarnation.

If we summarize what we have found, the result is that the New Testament does not conceive of the sacrifice of Christ as consisting only in his death. His whole life under the sign of the Suffering Servant of the Lord is filled with the idea of sacrifice. In reality his act of sacrifice extends back into the heavenly world; incarnation and sacrifice are inseparably connected. But this extension of the idea of sacrifice does not imply a minimizing of his death. The sacrifice is concentrated in his death. Death is not only the most

[3] Nygren, *op. cit.*, p. 60.

obvious and greater expression of the sacrifice; it is above all its fulfilment. Christ's act of sacrifice reaches its climax in the death on the cross. The cross gathers up and perfects all previous sacrifice. It does not mean simply that the Lord's earthly ministry is ended, it means that all "is finished." With this in mind we turn now to the question of the relation of the sacrifice to the risen and glorified Christ.

In our review of the various ecumenical contributions to the discussion about the Lord's Supper in Part I of this book, we found several statements concerning the continuous sacrifice of Christ in heaven. Thus Hicks: the sacrifice of Christ is a continuous sacrifice. He is still obedient as he sits on the right hand of God "for he is still man." We are lifted up into heaven and admitted to the heavenly worship which the Book of Revelation describes in chapters 4-7. Hebert: our High Priest continually performs his sacrifice at the heavenly altar. Dix: the eucharist is a manifestation in time of the eternal act of Christ as the heavenly High Priest at the altar before the throne of God, perpetually pleading his accomplished and effectual sacrifice. Pascher: the resurrection and the ascension also belong to Christ's sacrifice. "Through his resurrection and ascension he has entered the Holy of Holies and completes there eternally the offering of his body and blood." When some of these statements are taken literally, they suggest that the heavenly offering is a continuous extension of the sacrifice performed during Christ's earthly life and therefore of the same nature. The formulation given by Dix is more careful when he says that Christ pleads the sacrifice once made. Is it biblically legitimate to maintain a continuous offering of Christ in heaven? If we approach the New Teastament with this question, we may first of all establish two facts.

In the first place, through his resurrection and ascension Christ enters into an entirely new state. He lives no longer as the Suffering Servant of the Lord, but as the glorified Lord, sitting on the right hand of the Father. The distinction which an older theology used to make between the states of humiliation and exaltation has clear biblical support. The resurrection is God's yes to the sacrifice fulfilled in death. The ascension is the coronation of Christ: God "made him sit at his right hand in the heavenly places, far above all rule and authority and power and dominion, and above every name that is named, not only in this age but also in that which is to come" (Eph. 1:20-21). In view of these facts it seems difficult to find any meaning in the statement that the resurrection and the ascension belong to the sacrifice. It can be said that these events constitute the presentation of the sacrifice made once for all and God's acceptance of it, but not that they are a continuous offering. No matter how closely the New Testament combines the cross and the resurrection, the resurrection is something else than the sacrifice on the cross. The resurrection is the evidence of victory; it unveils and reveals that victory which lay hidden in the sacrifice of the cross.

In the second place, the ascension does not involve a separation. The ascended and glorified Lord does not cease to live in fellowship with those for whom he gave his life. This is indicated by the biblical statements which say that Christ is our advocate with the Father (I John 2:1), that Christ always lives to "make intercession" for us (Heb. 7:25), and that he appears "in the presence of God on our behalf" (Heb. 9:24). The witness to this fellowship with Christ is not confined to the individual passages which speak of the intercession of the heavenly High Priest for his own. It is implied in the conception of the church which is characteristic of the New Testament. Christ is inseparately united with his church, and the church with him. The living Lord is present in the church. The life of the church is participation in his life. Here is a relationship, a unity, which is exemplified in the statement that the church is designated as the body of Christ, and therefore also in a certain sense one with Christ himself.

We have seen, therefore, that the biblical authors strongly emphasize the difference between the earthly life of Jesus in the state of humiliation and his glorified existence in heaven; but that they also emphasize the solidarity and fellowship between the Lord and his church, which makes him really one with the church. With this twofold perspective as a starting point we turn to the question of the continuous sacrifice of Christ in heaven. The most important document to be considered in this connection is, of course, the Letter to the Hebrews.

According to the Letter to the Hebrews Christ is a high priest "forever according to the order of Melchizedek." His function as high priest has not ceased after the exaltation. "We have such a high priest, one who is seated at the right hand of the throne of the Majesty in heaven, a minister in the sanctuary and the true tent which is set up not by man but by the Lord" (Heb. 8:1-2). The function of a high priest is "to offer gifts and sacrifices; hence it is necessary for this priest also to have something to offer" (Heb. 8:3). In what sense does the Letter to the Hebrews speak here about a continuous sacrifice? Under any circumstances the suggestion that the heavenly "sacrifice" involves a repetition of or an addition to the sacrifice on the cross must be rejected. The author of the letter is clearly anxious to point out that the sacrifice of Christ is different from all the sacrifices made under the old covenant because this is made once for all. This phrase, "once for all," is repeated again and again. Christ did not need to offer repeated sacrifices, like the priests of the old covenant, for he "did this once for all when he offered up himself" (Heb. 7:27; cf. 9:25ff). "He entered once for all into the Holy Place . . . thus securing an eternal redemption" (Heb. 9:12). "But when Christ had offered for all time a single sacrifice for sins, he sat down at the right hand of God, then to wait until his enemies should be made a stool for his feet. For by a single offering he has perfected for all time those who are consecrated" (Heb. 10:12-14).

What kind of conception of the heavenly High Priest do we derive from these passages? As High Priest Christ has entered into the Holy Place. He brought that sacrifice of reconciliation which was made once for all and which implied an eternal redemption. That he remains a high priest forever according to the order of Melchizedek does not mean that he continually repeats the sacrifice he made during his earthly life. It means rather that this sacrifice made once for all is eternally valid. The new covenant of reconciliation has been established, and it remains on the basis of the sacrifice that has been made. Because Christ "holds his priesthood permanently . . . he is able for all time to save those who draw near to God through him, since he always lives to make intercession for them" (Heb. 7:24-25). These words point to the *koinonia* which exists between Christ and his church in which he saves fully those who draw near to God through him. We find here, therefore, a reflection of the characteristic conception of the church in the New Testament. The title High Priest plays the same part here as the title Messiah-Christ. As Messiah-Christ cannot be thought of as existing without his people, so neither can the heavenly High Priest exist without his church. When this High Priest makes his entrance into the heavenly world, he does not come alone. He comes in fellowship with those who belong to the new covenant established in his blood, and this fellowship expresses itself in his intercession for them.

If we want to call this intercession an "offering," we may do so in accordance with both Old Testament and current Christian usage. The Letter to the Hebrews, however, does not use this expression directly, but it says in a different connection that we are to "offer up a sacrifice of praise to God, that is, the fruit of lips that acknowledge his name" (Heb. 13:15). But even if neither the Letter to the Hebrews nor the rest of the New Testament speak directly of intercession as a sacrifice, there is no reason why we should reject a usage which has such broad biblical basis. But then what we must remember is that "sacrifice" is used in a different sense from the atoning sacrifice of Christ. The difference is apparent already in the fact that Christ's intercessory sacrifice is continuous, while the sacrifice through which God reconciled the world to himself has been made once for all. The intercessory sacrifice rests on the foundation of the sacrifice of reconciliation. The intercessory sacrifice is not designed to create a new covenant, but to realize the covenant which has already been established. Through his intercession the heavenly High Priest proclaims his solidarity with his church in all its wants and weakness. The purpose of his intercession is to release and actualize the powers of life which are contained in the atonement. The significance of the intercession becomes clearer if we compare the statements in the Letter to the Hebrews with the high priestly prayer of Jesus in John 17. What the Lord prays for is that the members of his church may be one as the Father and the Son are one, that they may be preserved from evil, and that they may be sanctified in truth. The background of this prayer is the act of reconciliation: "I glorified thee on earth, having accomplished the work which thou gavest me to do" (John 17:4). Since the prayer rests on the sacrifice of reconciliation, it is connected also with the unity of the Son with the Father and his fellowship with his church.

As a result of this discussion we may state that the sacrifice of reconciliation, which was made once for all, has been taken into heaven by the heavenly High Priest. This is something which happened in and with the exaltation of Christ, which also implies that God received the sacrifice. But this does not at all mean that the sacrifice now belongs to the past. The most essential factor is that the sacrifice is eternally valid and that it is continually relevant. It is continually present in the person of the heavenly High Priest. Furthermore, it may be biblical to speak of a sacrifice of intercession which the High Priest offers continually. To be sure, he is no longer the Suffering Servant of the Lord, as he was during his earthly life and in death. He is the exalted One who sits on the right hand of the Majesty on high. But in his exercise of his "eternal priesthood" he lives also in full fellowship with his church, and this fellowship expresses itself in his continuous intercession, which rests on the foundation of the atonement and the new covenant.

15

The Sacrifice and the Real Presence

In the previous chapters we have sought to clarify the position and significance of sacrifice in the New Testament. It has been necessary to do this because the fundamental conception of the sacrifice of Christ determines the view of the relationship of the sacrifice to the Lord's Supper. So far we have established only that there is a relationship and an inseparable connection between Holy Communion and the sacrifice of Christ perfected on the cross. We must now define more closely the nature of this relationship. In order to do so we must examine the idea of sacrifice in the Lord's Supper in connection with the presence of Christ in the sacrament, the real presence. These two factors are so closely related that, as the history of the doctrine of the sacrament indicates, a separation of the two leads to very serious consequences.

The New Testament consistently maintains the real presence of Christ in the eucharist. He is not present in a visible manner. It is the heavenly Christ who is invisibly present at this table fellowship, and who establishes a living relationship with his own. But the invisible Lord is at the same time the one who will return in a visible form. His presence now in the Lord's Supper is from one point of view an anticipation of his visible appearance in the Parousia and of the future glory. The Lord's Supper, as well as the whole Christian life in the primitive church, was pervaded by an expectant eschatology. The communion proclaims the Lord's death *until he comes*. The Lord's Supper here on earth points to the great supper in heaven. In a twofold sense the eucharist is an eschatological event. It is permeated by an expectant eschatology which expresses itself in the prayer: "Our Lord, come!" (*Maranatha*) (I Cor. 16:22). But at the same time it is characterized by what has been called "realized eschatology." The new age which has come in Christ "in the fulness of time" is often described as "the end of these days" (Heb. 1:1; I Pet. 1:20; I John 2:18). *Now*—there is always a strong emphasis on "now" in the New Testament—Christ is present in the Lord's Supper, and with him also the whole salvation which belongs to the new age. In this way the fulfilment and the expectation, the present and the future are joined together. We can apply to the Lord's Supper the words of the Letter to the Hebrews about those who have tasted the heavenly gift and the powers of the age to come (Heb. 6:4, 5).

The celebration of the eucharist in the primitive church was characterized by certainty of the presence of the Lord and of their constantly renewed fellowship with him. The basis for this fellowship, as we have already stated, was the resurrection and the ascension. Christ has not been separated from his own by the ascension. He has been exalted above the limitations of time and space, and therefore he can meet his own just as well in Corinth and Rome as in Jerusalem. What the Book of Revelation says in the letter to Laodicea indicates how they conceived of the Lord's presence in the eucharist: "Behold, I stand at the door and knock; if anyone hears my voice and opens the door, I will come in to him and eat with him, and he with me" (Rev. 3:20).

This view of the presence of Christ has a fundamental significance, and it is, as we have seen, common to all New Testament authors. We find it in Paul and John as well as in Acts. Thus Cullmann writes: "The idea that a fellowship is established with the risen Lord in the holy supper is the background of Paul's state-

ment in I Corinthians 10:14ff and also his words in 11:17."[1]
In its interpretation of the eucharist the Gospel of John emphasizes
that the Christ who is present in the sacrament is none other than
the Incarnate: the Word that became flesh and dwelt among us.
In the sixth chapter the evangelist evidently maintains that the
presence of Christ in the sacrament is as real as his physical presence was during the days of his flesh.[2]

But even though the ancient, eucharistic celebration rests on
the certainty of the presence of the risen and heavenly Lord, the
problem of the real presence is not thereby completely solved.
We have previously noted how the exaltation and the cross are
joined together in an inseparable unity. The question then is how
the real presence in the eucharist is related to the cross, or to the
act of voluntary sacrifice which characterized the Lord's earthly
life, and which was fulfilled in his "obedience unto death."

Our study began with a presentation of the modern discussion
about the eucharist, and we have come to a consideration of the
New Testament by way of the Reformation. With the variegated
history of the eucharist in mind we may at this point formulate the
question thus: What part do the "eucharistic elements" play in
relation to the presence of Christ? Has the New Testament in any
sense associated the Lord's presence with the bread and the wine?
This question naturally leads to a consideration of the words of
institution. We may start with the assertion already made that
according to these narratives the central content in this last supper
was the idea of sacrifice. It is not necessary for our purpose to
consider all the complicated, and possibly insoluble, exegetical
problems which are connected with these narratives of the institution of the sacrament. Under any circumstances it cannot be denied
that what the Lord did with the bread and the wine, and the words
which he spoke, even in their shortest form, point toward his

[1] Cullmann, op. cit., p. 99.
[2] Higgins, op. cit., p. 77.

approaching death, and also provide an interpretation of the redemptive significance of his death. What is about to happen is not merely a legal murder or a victory of the hostile powers; it is above all an act of sacrifice performed by the Suffering Servant of the Lord through which the victory is won and the new covenant of reconciliation between God and his people is established. The body of Christ is given, his blood is shed; this is the one, effective, perfect, and forever valid sacrifice, which supersedes the multitudes of ancient sacrifices. It is a vicarious sacrifice, and therefore results in the establishment of a covenant and the church. The eucharist of the last supper was not in itself a sacrifice, but it has nevertheless a sacrificial character, because everything is concentrated around that final, self-giving sacrifice which immediately followed.

When he gives the bread and the wine to them, the disciples become included in the sacrifice of Christ's death; they participate in its redemptive effects and in the *koinonia* of the new covenant. This participation is connected with the eating of the bread and the drinking of the wine. When the words of institution designate the bread as the body of Christ and wine as his blood, the meaning of this identification is perfectly clear. It is not a question of "transubstantiation" or "consubstantiation." In this connection all such ideas are excluded. The conceptions which these scholastic interpretations use do not and could not exist in the biblical texts which describe the Lord's last supper with his disciples. What the Lord says when he gives the bread and the wine to his disciples is that he gives himself, his body and blood, for them. The interpretive words do not speak about something that is to happen to the bread and the wine, but about that which will happen to him. By the giving of the bread and the wine he actualizes the sacrifice which immediately follows and thereby also the whole mystery of redemption included in that sacrifice. What happens involves an anticipation of that which is going to happen; yes, the sacrifice about to take place becomes a present reality in that which happens in the last supper.

In this way, therefore, the sacrifice is inseparably united with the Holy Communion. There may be a difference of opinion in regard to the authenticity of the words "do this in remembrance of me." These words are not present in the account in Mark. But even if they were not spoken on that last evening Jesus spent with his disciples, it is nevertheless proper to point out that the idea of a repetition is in accordance with Jesus' intention and belongs to the very nature of the last supper.[3] The celebration of the eucharist in the ancient church differs from that which happened on the last evening because Christ is no longer present in a visible manner, and the sacrifice on the cross now belongs to the past. But this does not involve a curtailment of the presence or a setting aside of sacrifice. The place Jesus had at that last supper is now occupied by the living, heavenly Lord. The ascension is the condition of his continuing presence. The sacrifice of Christ does not belong only to the past. The sacrifice fulfilled once for all is eternally valid, and as such it is effectively present in the sacrament. In this way Christ mediates the blessings of the new covenant to the new people of God.

When we listen to Paul, we find this basic view developed in the characteristic Pauline formulations. The Lord's Supper involves a participation in the sacrifice of Christ and therefore also fellowship with Christ. It may be significant that in I Corinthians 10:16 Paul begins to talk about the cup and participation in the blood of Christ. "The cup of blessing which we bless, is it not a participation in the blood of Christ?" With these words about the blood of Christ the attention is first called to participation in the sacrifice of Christ. In this connection we are reminded of what the apostle writes in Philippians 3:10, how he has suffered the loss of all things "that I may know him and the power of his

---

[3] Cf. Riesenfeld, "Nattvarden," p. 30; Higgins, *op. cit.,* p. 55.

resurrection, and may share his sufferings." This participation which Paul describes as an individual experience becomes valid in the Lord's Supper for the whole church. When Paul passes on to the bread, he designates this as a participation in the body of Christ, and proceeds to speak of the unity of the church. "Because there is one loaf, we who are many are one body, for we all partake of the same loaf." The primary factor is participation in Christ; then follows the unity of the church. As frequently in Paul, the expression, "the body of Christ," has a twofold meaning: it refers both to Christ himself and to his church. The idea of sacrifice is present here also, even if not quite as markedly as in Paul's words about the blood. Participation in the body of Christ involves sharing in that which happened to his human body, i.e. in the suffering that accompanied his voluntary act of sacrifice.[4] According to Paul's interpretation the bread and wine are the vehicles through which the guests at the table become participants in the body and blood of Christ. Christ has tied his redemptive presence in the sacrament to these means. Paul's conception is illustrated by the parallel which he draws in I Corinthians 10 between the eucharist and the food and drink which Israel received during their wandering in the wilderness. "All ate the same supernatural food and all drank the same supernatural drink. For they drank from the supernatural Rock which followed them, and the Rock was Christ" (I Cor. 10:3-4). The eucharistic bread and wine are the "spiritual food and drink" which Christ gives to his own.

Does the Gospel of John differ from this view of the bread and the wine as the means and vehicles to which the Lord has attached his redemptive presence in the sacrament? What significance do such words as these have: "Unless you eat the flesh of the Son of man and drink his blood, you have no life in you" (John 6:53)?

It is quite natural that the attitude of the Gospel of John to the Lord's Supper should be subject to widely different interpreta-

[4] Higgins, *op. cit.*, p. 70.

tions. Even today there are prominent exegetes who hold that John's attitude to the sacraments is relatively passive. In general, however, exegetical development has gone in the opposite direction. Sacramental conceptions and allusions have been found everywhere in the Gospel. It is difficult at any rate to avoid the judgment that the positive point of view is closer to the truth than the negative. At the same time it is clear that John speaks of these things in veiled and ambiguous language. Ramsey is no doubt correct in his interpretation of John 6. "Even if it were true that this chapter does not refer to the eucharist but to the whole work of Christ whose incarnation feeds the souls of men, it nevertheless shows the place of the eucharist in Christianity just as strongly as if its reference were more directly eucharistic. For the language of 'bread' and 'eating' and of 'blood' and 'drinking' is the Christian's eucharistic language, and to express the Incarnation in the language of the eucharist betokens the importance of the rite just as emphatically as to express the eucharist in terms of the Incarnation." [5] In reality there can be no doubt but that the evangelist in writing the sixth chapter had the sacrament in mind. On the basis of the last words in verse 51 regarding the bread which Jesus gives for the life of the world, Dodd, who emphasizes John's habit of speaking in ambiguous terms, says that, if the question of "how" were raised, John would have answered in sacramental terms.[6]

John's interpretation of that which is food indeed and drink indeed is a part of the fundamental theme which is governed by the idea of the incarnation: The Word became flesh. Jesus is "the bread of life." This bread "comes down from heaven" and gives eternal life. The fathers ate manna in the wilderness and died. But he who eats of this bread shall never die; he already has eternal life and the promise of a resurrection on the last day. "For my flesh is food indeed, and my blood is drink indeed. He who eats my flesh and drinks my blood abides in me, and I in him."

[5] Ramsey, op. cit., p. 106.   [6] Cf. Dodd, op. cit., pp. 133ff, 333ff.

There is an obvious parallelism between the incarnation and the life-giving presence of the Lord in the sacramental bread. In both instances divine glory, *doxa,* appears in the guise of humility. The Word who became flesh appears in the lowliness of humanity, and the life-giving Lord appears in the lowly bread. In both there is an implied miracle which causes offense, "a stumbling block," "a hard saying." "The Jews" murmured at the saying that the Lord had come down from heaven, i.e. the incarnation. They knew "his father and mother." And many of his disciples murmured at the saying that they must eat the flesh of the Son of man and drink his blood. In both of these connections the Gospel speaks, therefore, of the necessity of faith. Eating and drinking do not give eternal life automatically. "He who *believes* has eternal life." But man himself cannot produce faith. "No one can come to me unless it is granted him by the Father." "This is the work of God, that you believe in him whom he has sent."

Even if the first part of the discourse about the bread of life which follows the feeding of the five thousand only indirectly deals with the Lord's Supper, there can be no question but that the latter part from verse 51 on is related to the celebration of the sacrament in the ancient church. What conception of the real presence and the sacrifice do we gain from this section?

That the Son of man gives his "body and blood" as food and drink evidently means that he gives himself to his own. "Body and blood" is not some material apart from Christ himself, it is his own personal presence. This gift includes therefore "eternal life" and a promise of a resurrection "on the last day." This gift of life is bestowed in and with the union with Christ. "He who eats my flesh and drinks my blood abides in me, and I in him." The Christ who is actively present in the eucharistic bread and wine is the risen and glorified Lord. This identity is in reality quite obvious and directly affirmed in verse 62, when he says that the Son of man will return to "where he was before." The ascension is the necessary presupposition of the risen Lord's presence in the sacrament. But this presence of the living Lord is inseparably connected with the sacrifice of Christ. Cullmann points out that the word "give" (*didomi*, vs. 51) has a twofold meaning: distribute, and give up to death.[7] I quote a few words from Dodd's commentary on the Fourth Gospel: "Yet the expression 'to give his flesh,' however figuratively it is taken, can hardly fail to suggest the idea of death. And the expression 'to drink the blood,' again, can hardly fail to suggest shed blood, and therefore violent death. In such veiled terms the evangelist suggests that it is through death that Christ becomes bread of life to the world."[8] We may add that the reference here is not only to the sacrifice once perfected in death. The expression, "to drink my blood," suggests that the living Lord makes his own participate in his sacrifice and in its redemptive and life-giving power, so that the sacrifice even in this sense becomes relevant and present.

In these Johannine, eucharistic texts the elements seem to receive a stronger emphasis than anywhere else in the New Testament. Nowhere else do we read about eating the flesh and drinking the blood of the Son of man. Furthermore John accentuates the point by using the term *sarx* rather than the more usual *soma,* and the word which he uses for "eat" is the very expressive Greek verb *trogein* which means to chew or to masticate. All these factors are congruent with the strongly anti-docetic attitude which characterizes the Johannine writings. In sharp contrast to all docetic Christology John emphasizes that the Word became flesh (*sarx*) and that divine glory (*doxa*) meets us in lowly humanity. The evangelist brings this fundamental thought to bear also on the Lord's Supper, and he does so with an intensity and realism which is unmistakable. He chooses his terms with the intention to shock and cause offense.

[7] Cullmann, *op. cit.,* p. 99.
[8] Dodd, *op. cit.,* 339

But in spite of this emphasis he also says: "It is the spirit that gives life, the flesh is of no avail." It is understandable that many find it difficult to reconcile these two points of view. On the one hand it is absolutely necessary to eat the flesh of the Son of man, and on the other hand the flesh is of no avail. But in reality there is no contradiction here. The real relationship between these seemingly contradictory statements has been admirably clarified by Cullmann. "Because the fourth evangelist, unlike all the others, stresses the divinity of the Logos and because he accordingly says, in this chapter on the Eucharist (v. 63), that the decisive, life-giving element is not the flesh, not the *sarx* but the Spirit, the *pneuma,* just because of these things, this evangelist has endeavored more than any other to avoid the misleading conclusion which could be drawn from this that the flesh, the *sarx,* as medium of the working of the Spirit, is therefore not really to be taken seriously. . . . On the basis of the ascension, the Spirit is now at work, and in the flesh, the reality of which is to be taken absolutely seriously, although it is *not the flesh* which 'giveth life,' for the flesh (in itself) 'profiteth nothing' (v. 63). There is no contradiction between the crude expression 'to eat the flesh' and the phrase 'the flesh is of no avail'; on the contrary this antithesis is entirely in keeping with the basic thought of John's Gospel." [9]

There is no inner contradiction in John's interpretation of the Lord's Supper. Obviously, however, it is characterized by a two-fold contrast. On the one hand John is opposed to a docetic point of view which denies "that Jesus Christ has come in the flesh" (I John 4:2), and on the other hand he rejects the idea of "eating the god" which was prevalent in the mystery cults. The words about the spirit that gives life and the flesh that is of no avail exclude this latter idea. The presence of Christ in the Lord's Supper is the presence of the living and life-giving Lord. But this heavenly Christ is no one else than he "who came in the

[9] Cullmann, *op. cit.,* p. 100.

flesh." The presence of Christ is therefore tied to the sacrifice, as is indicated through the words about eating the flesh of the Son of man and drinking his blood. In and through this sacrifice the living Lord bestows the gift of eternal life. The uniqueness of the Gospel of John is clearly evident. But the fundamental point of view is nevertheless in complete harmony with what the rest of the New Testament says about the presence and the sacrifice. The New Testament speaks, as it were, with different dialects, but the language is nevertheless the same.

Before we leave the New Testament, we must consider one more question. In the preceding discussion we have frequently encountered the problem of the relationship between the celebration of the eucharist in the Christian church and "the service in the heavenly sanctuary." It has been said, for instance, that at our earthly worship we are admitted to that heavenly service which the Book of Revelation describes. In a frequently used formula the statement is made that the great High Priest brings his sacrifice to the heavenly altar in this heavenly worship. We remember also that the report of the ecumenical meeting at Lund in 1952 was satisfied merely to define various attitudes on this point. "Some," it states, talk about our sacrifice only as an offering of praise, thanksgiving, and obedient service, while "others" would insist that "in the Holy Eucharist the Lord Jesus Christ as God's Great High Priest unites the oblation made by His body, the Church, with His own sacrifice, and so takes up her own adoration into the *Sanctus* of the company of heaven." It further notes that between these two extremes there are other views "to which a brief reference may not do full justice."

The formulations of the two alternatives given here do not give us a clear idea of what separates them. The second alternative has been formulated in such a way that it is difficult to understand why it should not have received more general acceptance. Nothing in this statement indicates that any other kind of sacrifice is intended than that spoken of in the first alternative. What is said about the action of the great High Priest would not in itself cause any objection. The thought that the Lord includes his church in his sacrifice, and that he in solidarity with his church unites its prayers in his high priestly prayer and its praise with "the *Sanctus* of the company of heaven," does not stand in conflict with the message of the New Testament. It would seem, therefore, that the antitheses which may have been the background of the two statements have in reality been concealed.

It would be completely foreign to the biblical conception, however, if we should regard the Lord's Supper as our offering of Christ. In connection with the eucharist the New Testament speaks of our thanksgiving and prayer. It is also evident that the *koinonia* which is given in and with the sacrament must express itself in "obedient service." In these connections the New Testament uses the term sacrifice only occasionally. We might refer here to Romans 12:1, where Paul admonishes his brethren "to present your bodies as a living sacrifice, holy and acceptable to God," and to Hebrews 13:15, where the author uses an Old Testament quotation in urging the congregation to "offer up a sacrifice of praise," after which he adds: "Do not neglect to do good and to share what you have, for such sacrifices are pleasing to God." If, in traditional terminology, we want to speak of our thanksgiving, prayer, and service as "an offering," we must realize that this "offer" is not a free and independent effort on our part, but that it rests completely on the sacrifice of his love and has been produced by the power of his Spirit. But we look in vain for any New Testament statement to the effect that we "offer Christ." It is good New Testament doctrine that Christ incorporates his church into his sacrifice, and that it shares in the blessing he has obtained. That we thus receive the sacrament in faith means that we entrust ourselves to him who has given himself for us. But this is something radically different from our offering Christ or his sacrifice. Christ has offered himself once for all. No man has ever offered or will ever offer Christ. The sacrifice is his own act, and the act of God who gave his only Son.

It would also be foreign to the thought of the New Testament if we were to interpret the offering of the heavenly High Priest "in the heavenly sanctuary" as a continuous offering similar to the sacrifice on the cross. The poetic and beautiful picture of Christ bringing his offering to the heavenly sanctuary can easily be interpreted in that direction. It seems to suggest that Christ continues to present an atoning sacrifice before God. In this connection reference is sometimes made to the description of the heavenly worship in the Book of Revelation, but this passage does not provide any support for this view. It does not suggest that "the Lamb" is still being offered. On the contrary it says, "Worthy is the Lamb who *was* slain to receive power and wealth and wisdom and might and honor and glory and blessing!" The Lamb has conquered and now together with God receives adoration from all creation. "To him who sits upon the throne and to the Lamb be blessing and honor and glory and might for ever and ever!" (Rev. 5:9-14). In regard to the high priestly function of Christ in heaven we may say by way of summation that it can be understood from two points of view. 1) During his early life Christ has once for all made the perfect sacrifice in his death. This sacrifice is eternally valid and therefore also eternally present. On this basis Christ is forever the great, heavenly High Priest. 2) When in addition the New Testament speaks of a continuous, high priestly "offering," it does not refer to that atoning sacrifice through which he has created the new age and established the new order (Eph. 1:10), but rather to the intercession which the heavenly High Priest in solidarity with his church makes in order that the work of redemption may be realized on earth, and his church may become pure and sanctified.

The connection between earthly and heavenly worship was no

doubt very vividly conceived of in the ancient church. In this connection it is customary to speak of earthly worship as a "copy" of the heavenly, usually with a reference to visions of that heavenly worship found in the Book of Revelation. Naturally these visions are described more or less against the background of the worship service in the ancient church. It is no doubt true, as Riesenfeld says, that psychologically the actual cultus is primary in relation to the visions, but theologically the thought is that heavenly worship is "the essential reality of which the gatherings of the Christian church are a copy." [10]

Even if we are concerned here with viewpoints which were essential to the ancient church, we must not expect too much of this fragmentary material. It is above all important to see the relationship between the heavenly and the earthly services of worship in the context of what the New Testament in general says about the new relationship between heaven and earth established in Christ. Paul says in Ephesians 1:3 that God "has blessed us in Christ with every spiritual blessing in the heavenly places," and again in 2:6, God "has raised us up with him, and made us sit with him in the heavenly places in Christ Jesus." These and many other similar statements show that the idea of "a copy" of something very far away, even if it is somewhat significant, does not express fully the New Testament conception of the relationship between heavenly and earthly worship.

If we do speak of worship on earth as a copy or an echo of heavenly worship, it must be primarily from the point of view of the worship service as a eucharist. Heavenly worship is primarily praise. What the Seer in the Apocalypse saw and heard was that paean of praise which was sung by the worshiping multitude. These visions call attention to something which is essential also in worship on earth. But the word "copy" does not tell us everything about the relationship between heavenly worship and earthly wor-

[10] Riesenfeld, "Kristen gudstjänst," p. 59.

ship. That which is of paramount importance is that Christ himself, and with him "every spiritual blessing in the heavenly places," is present in worship on earth and there actualizes the sacrifice in which he gave himself for us and through which he unites us to himself. The meaning of what happens when we celebrate the Lord's Supper "in the name of Jesus" is that heaven opens and, as it were, descends on us, so that our worship becomes worship in communion with "the whole company of heaven." This comprehensive view of the fellowship which embraces "the heavenly host" and all the saints of God in heaven appears very clearly in the New Testament. I refer especially to the remarkable words in the Letter to the Hebrews. "But you have come to Mount Zion and to the city of the living God, the heavenly Jerusalem, and to innumerable angels in festal gathering, and to the assembly of the first-born who are enrolled in heaven, and to a judge who is God of all, and to the spirits of just men made perfect, and to Jesus, the mediator of a new covenant, and to the sprinkled blood that speaks more graciously than the blood of Abel" (Heb. 12:22-24). Heavenly worship is tied together with that on earth.[11] Christ, *Kyrios,* officiates as the heavenly High Priest in the worship of the church and there he makes his own participants in the blood which "speaks more graciously" than that of Abel. The worshiping congregation may therefore "with confidence draw near to the throne of grace" (Heb. 4:16).

[11] Cf. W. Hahn, *Gottesdienst und Opfer Christi,* (1951), p. 108; and William Manson, *The Epistle to the Hebrews* (London: Hodder & Stoughton, 1951), p. 122.

Part IV

Conclusions

16

Ecumenical Orientation

If we ask what are the most remarkable and sensational events in church history during the present century, the answer must be: the appearance of younger churches in non-Christian countries and the ecumenical movement. Even if we hold that the results of ecumenical efforts have been rather meager, and even if we consider all the difficulties confronting the movement, we insist that what has happened has created a new situation both in church life and in theology. The earlier isolation between the various communions has broken down. New contacts have been made. There has been a reversal of the current. The development proceeds no longer in the direction of a growing fragmentation, as was true for centuries, but rather in the direction of a growing fellowship.

It is obvious that theology cannot remain oblivious to this change. "Ecumenicity" places new demands on theology, and at the same time provides it with new possibilities. In this situation the most important element is not the great conferences, although they, too, are significant, but the continuous and expanding conversations which theologians from different schools of thought carry on in regard to central theological problems. Such conversations across confessional boundaries have never before appeared in the history of theology. We are therefore justified in speaking of a new theological situation. The situation which was created by the Reformation and which has persisted through the centuries may be characterized as "trench warfare." Each one maintained his own position. The relationship to other communions was mostly polemic. The whole situation had become stereotyped and immovable. The theological formulations were regarded as having been fixed once for all. Wherever any discussion was held, the subject consisted of the formulations rather than the religious reality expressed in them.

The struggle in regard to the Lord's Supper was carried on in this fashion for centuries. Lutheran theology in its opposition to Rome repeated continually Luther's polemic against the Roman doctrine and practice of the mass as these appeared at the time of the Reformation. In the same way Lutheran theologians contended against the Reformed doctrine with weapons taken from Luther's discussion with Zwingli at Marburg. As a standard in this war on two fronts they advanced the scholastic formula, "consubstantiation." This polemic theology paid no heed to the Roman claim that the conception under attack was a corrupted form of the sacrament which was far removed from the Augustinian-Thomist line in Roman theology. The intense struggle against the Reformed conception was conducted on similar lines. If in the case of Rome the polemic was against corruption, in the case of the Reformed it was against impoverishment. They argued as if the Reformed, Calvinist doctrine of the Lord's Supper was nothing else than a spiritual dissolution of the sacrament.

It was, of course, not only Lutheran theology which carried on this stereotyped polemic. Roman and even Reformed theology was similarly affected. We need not pursue this subject any further. Rome has frequently demonstrated its complete inability to understand that religious factors were the primary cause of the Reformation. This attitude determined its polemic. Reformed theology, on the other hand, has through the centuries maintained its view of the Lutheran Reformation in general and its doctrine of the eucharist in particular as nothing but a compromise and an attempt to be on both sides of the fence.

In principle, even if not always yet in practice, a polemic of this type belongs to the past. Many factors have contributed to this situation, lately also the ecumenical movement. The traditional battle lines have become meaningless. It is meaningless to keep on attacking positions which the opponent refuses to acknowledge as his own. But if the traditional, confessional struggles have ceased, it does not mean that the confessional antitheses have become less important or even unessential. The ecumenical movement would disappear if it were to seek to obtain results by relativizing the demand for truth.

What does it mean then for theology to become ecumenically oriented? It means willingness to associate, to learn to know one another, to learn from one another, to make critical self-examinations, to maintain integrity in all relationships, and above all to obey in common the Spirit who "leads us into all the truth." Two attitudes become impossible. On the one hand, self-satisfied confessionalism, which is sufficient unto itself, refuses to listen to others, is unprepared for critical self-examination, and arrogantly pronounces its judgments as if the last word had been spoken, must be abandoned. On the other hand, we cannot maintain an attitude which finds a solution by smoothing over differences, uncritically combines diverse elements, proceeds with the idea of accommodation, and is indifferent to its own confessional standpoint because in reality it is indifferent to the demand of truth. The first is the standpoint of isolationism, the second does not inspire respect and leads only to confusion.

It is obvious that the ecumenical movement must be concerned with extending and strengthening fellowship even in theology. From the very beginning it was considered important to find a "basis" on which the negotiations could be conducted. At the two earlier conferences on Faith and Order at Lausanne in 1927 and at

Edinburgh in 1937, the primary object was a confrontation which would result in the recognition and definition of similarities and differences. Sometimes these differences were defined in reference to specific denominations; at other times it was stated that "some say," "others say," without indicating who these "some" and "others" were. The reason for this was partly that differences did not always coincide with denominational lines. This method of defining what unites and separates was justified as a starting point, and was, strictly speaking, inevitable during the early days of the ecumenical movement. But obviously it could be nothing more than the first stage, the confrontation. It has been rightly said that the conference in Lund marked the beginning of a new stage. To be sure, even in the report from this conference we find the old formula: "some say, others say." Nevertheless the chief tendency in Lund was in the direction of trying to overcome this ecumenical deadlock.

On the basis of experience up to that time it became clear that growth in fellowship could be attained only by a common and deeper study of biblical documents, about whose authority there were no differences of opinion. Such a reference to the Bible should not at all be surprising. But it is worth noting that the demand for this new biblical orientation came at a time when study of the Bible had established contacts across confessional boundaries and had therefore ceased being guided completely by confessional standards.

But Christianity has not only a universally accepted and authoritative Bible, it has also a common history which with few exceptions lasted down to the separation between East and West. The attitude of the communions to this undivided church has been variable. The Eastern Orthodox church regards itself as the direct continuation of this undivided church and as the legitimate guardian of this heritage. The decisions which were made by the seven ecumenical councils of the ancient church stand as authoritative tradition, in a certain sense on a par with the Bible. During the last century some theologians within the Church of England have strongly emphasized continuity with the ancient church. Lutheran and Reformed communions have incorporated the christological and trinitarian confessions of the ancient church in their own confessions. This has emphasized the connection with the ancient church, but it has not guaranteed closer contact with ancient tradition or a positive appreciation of it. This lack of contact has been a weakness which has contributed to the isolation and to an overemphasis on separate tradition. In reality the connection between the Reformation and the ancient church was stronger than that found in later theology.

But even if the contact with the ancient church must be regarded as an asset, and therefore also a significant ecumenical factor, the tradition of the ancient church cannot be regarded as a norm and still less as an authority on a par with the Bible. This tradition is not at all a finished and unanimous entity. The theological testimony of the undivided church contains not only variations but also disparate elements. This tradition, too, must be examined and verified in the light of the primary witness of the Bible. There are abundant examples of how biblical thoughts and viewpoints have been presented in an original and comprehensive manner by theologians in the ancient church, often in a bitter struggle against conceptions foreign to the Bible. It is difficult to overestimate what the ancient church has produced in this respect. But we can also find misinterpretations of and departures from biblical concepts, and even inability to preserve what is essential in the New Testament message. Appraisal of the theology of the ancient church and its contribution has suffered because conceptions belonging to a much later time have been read into ancient documents. Roman theologians, for instance, have appealed to ancient patristic literature to a greater extent than is warranted by the statements of the fathers themselves. This method of reading

later conceptions into these ancient documents have caused the
Protestants to take a much more negative attitude toward the
ancient church. This was especially the case during the period
of liberal theology, when even the ancient, christological confessions were regarded as products of a "hellenizing process," although in reality they were the opposite: they maintained the
ancient confession of Christ in opposition to hellenistic misinterpretations.

The plan of this book does not call for a comprehensive review
of the doctrine and liturgy of the Lord's Supper in the ancient
church. We must limit ourselves to a reference to two men in the
ancient church, Irenaeus and Cyprian. The first one was undoubtedly the greatest of the theologians of the first centuries,
and the second was one of the most influential.

In the interpretation of Irenaeus we find typical examples of
the tendency to read later ideas into ancient texts. This is true
both of Irenaeus' conception of the church and of his doctrine of
the Lord's Supper. When Irenaeus, for example, speaks of a
successio episcoporum, he has been interpreted as holding the later
Roman theory of episcopal ordination as a prerequisite for a valid
celebration of the eucharist. In reality the thoughts and theology
of Irenaeus stand in opposition to gnostic teachings. He does not
hold that a special grace of office is mediated through the succession. Instead, against the pretentions of the Gnostics of having a
special and secret tradition and esoteric truth apart from the
church, he maintains that the genuine tradition from the days of
the apostles is to be found within the church; and he bases his contention on the fact that the names of the bishops who have served
the congregations since that time are well known. Apostolic succession, according to Irenaeus, is therefore the succession of the
pure, apostolic doctrine.[1]

[1] Gustaf Wingren, *Människan och inkarnationen enligt Irenaeus* (Lund,
1947), p. 198.

Irenaeus' interpretation of the eucharist has been subjected to the same misinterpretation. G. Wingren writes: Irenaeus "presents the Lord's Supper as the pure sacrifice of the new covenant which replaces the sacrificial system of the Old Testament. Protestant authors are prone to underestimate the significance of the sacrifice, while Roman authors readily read later ideas from the doctrine of the mass into Irenaeus' writings." [2] When Irenaeus speaks of a sacrifice which the church offers in the eucharist, he does not imply that we in some way should offer Christ. In this connection Irenaeus thinks rather of the bread and the wine as the gifts of creation which the congregation brings before God to be used in the celebration. Such a presentation of "gifts and offerings" has no meritorious significance. The thought of the sacrifice of Christ occurs in a different connection. When Christ meets us in the bread and wine and thereby gives to us his body and blood, his action here is inseparably connected with his sacrifice. We could say both that sacrifice is the basis of the idea of communion, and that it is a part of this idea. In his struggle against the Gnostics and their denial of "the resurrection of the body" Irenaeus emphasized the significance of this communion with the body of Christ for eternal hope and for "the resurrection body." It would be wrong to posit here a conflict between spirit and body, and to interpret Irenaeus' theology as "physical" in contrast to spiritual. Man, says Irenaeus, receives nourishment through participation in the body of Christ, and "his growth, therefore," as Wingren says, "develops into the spiritual body, the resurrection body, in which the earthly struggle between sin and the Spirit, the flesh and the Spirit, ends in the victory of the Spirit. The Spirit will then have complete possession of the material, just as the resurrection of Christ is the complete domination of the *Spirit* over the humanity of Jesus and therefore also a resurrection of the *body*. . . . The Spirit will conclude his creative work in the resurrection and

[2] *Ibid.*, p. 195.

eternal life, when the Spirit, i.e., Life, penetrates the body." [3] Irenaeus' eucharistic theology has a very strong eschatological emphasis. His theology looks toward the dawn.

Cyprian's place in the history of the eucharist is a matter of controversy. This is not at all strange. In his writings we encounter for the first time the expression, "the suffering of Christ is the offering which we offer" in the eucharist. Ramsey discusses very interestingly the significance of this statement in its historical context. It is well to note what he has to say. We have touched upon this matter previously, but we must now examine it in more detail. According to Ramsey it is really not a question of anything new. His contention is that when Cyprian speaks of the body and blood of Christ as a sacrifice, "he simply states what is inherent in the eucharist just because it is inherent in Christ himself." Let us first see how Ramsey justifies this statement. He points out that prior to Cyprian the sacrifice in the eucharist was spoken of in various ways. Justin regards the sacrifice in the eucharist as thanksgiving and praise. Irenaeus thinks of it as the bread and the wine which are offered as the first fruits of creation. But among these men of the ancient church we find also some more profound suggestions. For Justin the rite commemorates the passion and the whole incarnate life of Jesus. Irenaeus connects the eucharist with Christ as the High Priest in heaven. When we consider the statement of Cyprian in this perspective, we must not isolate the eucharistic terminology but observe what place the sacrifice has in the work of Christ and in the life of the church, his body. Christ is present in heaven as a sacrifice, and his presence in the eucharist must be of the same nature. He is present as one who gave himself on the cross, and who there and then with his self-giving unites his people to his Father in heaven. The unique act of Christ in history is the source of what the church as the body of Christ does in the eucharist. When we realize all this, we understand that the sacrifice,

[3] *Ibid.*, pp. 185ff., 188.

connected first to bread and wine and to the prayers and praises of Christians, must be applied finally to the body and blood of Christ.[4]

According to Ramsey's argument Cyprian's interpretation of the sacrifice is the legitimate result of the development within the ancient church. He maintains that everything points forward to Cyprian's interpretation of the sacrifice. But Ramsey is well aware of the perils connected with this interpretation of the sacrifice. We have already noted his argument that abuses may arise under three different conditions. It happens, in the first place, when the sacrifice is identified exclusively with death and destruction. This identification led to the Medieval conception of the mass as a repetition of the sacrifice on Golgotha. In the second place, misinterpretations arise when the action of Christ is separated from that of the Father, as if Christ were propitiating an estranged Father on man's behalf. In the third place, it occurs when the activity of the priest is separated from the one body, the church, and the priest as an individual and in virtue of rights inherent in himself offers in each mass a separate sacrifice to God.[5]

When we examine this argument, we cannot object to what Ramsey says about the necessity of considering the sacrifice in the eucharist in connection with the place which the thought of sacrifice has in the gospel message in general. Nor is there any reason to dispute his statement that the presence of Christ in the eucharist involves the presence of his sacrifice. But these considerations do not at all imply that this sacrifice is one that we, the church, offer. That the presence of Christ in the eucharist also makes his sacrifice present is not the same as saying that the church "offers" the body and blood of Christ. The latter statement would be true and verified only on the supposition that we completely identify Christ and the church. Now it is true that nothing more important can

[4] Ramsey, op. cit., p. 114ff.
[5] Ibid., p. 117.

be said of the church than that it is the body of Christ, which implies that Christ identifies himself with his church. But the profound truth of this statement does not permit us to turn this statement around and say that the church is Christ. If this last statement were valid, and if we thus identified the action of the church with Christ's own action, we could without difficulty say that the church offers Christ. The offering of the church would then be identical with Christ's own sacrifice. But if the sacrifice made by Christ once for all is primary in relation to the church, this identification becomes impossible. The sacrifice of Christ is and remains his own sacrifice, eternally valid, present in the eucharist, but entirely his own, not the church's sacrifice.

It is impossible, therefore, to interpret Cyprian's theory of sacrifice as the fulfilment of earlier thoughts about sacrifice, or as the goal toward which the previous development had moved. The peril of which Ramsey speaks is already present in Cyprian's formulation. In this connection we must point out that we find in Cyprian's teaching on the atonement something of the separation between the work of Christ and the Father, which Ramsey correctly regards as a starting point for misinterpretations of the idea of sacrifice in the eucharist. The difference in this respect between Cyprian and Irenaeus is obvious. For the latter the unity in the work of the Father and the Son is a living and obvious fact which he describes with many expressive figures. There is a connection between Cyprian's inability to see how the Father works in the Son and his view of the eucharistic sacrifice as our offering of the sacrifice of Christ. But having said this, we must add that there is a long development from Cyprian to the Medieval theories of the mass. If we were to find these theories in Cyprian's writings, we would read into the writings of this church father ideas which belong to a much later time. What we have in Cyprian is a vague and ambiguous formula, but nevertheless a formula which has had great significance for the later history of the eucharist.

These brief examples of interpretations of the eucharist in the ancient church demonstrate the peril of reading the views of a later age into the literature of the ancient church. They have also shown that we can learn both what is right and what is wrong from what happened in the church. It is clear that we must confront the interpretation of the Lord's Supper in the ancient church, as well as in all subsequent periods, with the testimony of the New Testament.

In the attempt we made in the previous section to view the eucharistic sacrifice in the light of the New Testament we sought to present the sacrifice in connection with the work of Christ as a whole, and also therefore in the context of the biblical conception of the church. We have also endeavored to place the sacrifice in the context of what the New Testament has to say about the significance of the Lord's Supper. We have found how inseparably the idea of sacrifice is united with the celebration of the sacrament in the ancient church, how central its position is, and how it is interwoven with other ideas in the sacrament. It is really surprising what an abundance of eucharistic ideas are to be found in the relatively few texts which deal with the Lord's Supper.

The New Testament puts its own critical questions to the various communions and to all later interpretations of the Lord's Supper. This gives us an occasion for self-examination. But even though the New Testament is the final authority, we do not find in it a definitely formulated doctrine which might be made the standard for the various interpretations of the Lord's Supper. What we have in the New Testament is not a regularly fixed and finally formulated doctrine of the Lord's Supper, but rather a series of different perspectives, a series of eucharistic motifs, which appear in a distinct context in redemptive history, from which they cannot be separated without losing their significance. These various eucharistic motifs may be likened to talents which the church of Christ has received to use and administer. They can be used in such a way that their treasures become more and more visible, but they can also be buried in the ground or traded for worthless coin. It is the function of the New Testament to propose critical questions. In reality this critical function begins within the New Testament. Both Paul and John exercise this function. In John there is a two-fold demarcation: against docetic spiritualism and against gross materialization. This twofold demarcation, however, is significant not only for New Testament times. It provides a guide also in regard to the subsequent history of the Lord's Supper.

17

Eucharist and Sacrifice

In our review of ecumenical discussions about the Lord's Supper we found that from a theological point of view these discussions revolve around the idea of sacrifice. It was found that the differences of opinion concerned especially the position and significance of this idea, as the report of the conference in Lund indicates. Since the time of the Edinburgh Conference, where the document by Hicks was presented, ecumenical literature, especially Anglican contributions, has spoken of a deadlock from which we must escape. What does this "deadlock" mean? If we follow the Anglican reasoning, we may say by way of a preliminary answer that sacrifice occupies a prominent place in the interpretation of the Lord's Supper which follows the "catholic" tradition, while it has lost its significance or become a secondary matter in the tradition from the Reformation. This negative attitude and the fear of speaking of sacrifice in connection with the Lord's Supper have been the results, it is claimed, of the polemic, legitimate in itself, against the doctrine of the mass.

One chief intention of the Anglican contributions to the ecumenical discussion of the Lord's Supper is to overcome the deadlock into which these discussions have bogged down. They want to do full justice to the Reformation, and at the same time preserve the so-called catholic tradition. Let us recall the reasoning through which they hope to reach this goal. The argumentation may appear in various forms, but essentially there is a common agreement.

185

They find the chief reason for the deadlock in the fact that Medieval theology associated the sacrifice of Christ exclusively with his death on the cross. This identification of his sacrifice with his death is the background of the theory that the sacrifice in the sacrament is a repetition of the sacrifice on Golgotha. Medieval theologians could not think of the presence of the sacrifice of Christ in the Lord's Supper in any other way. The Reformers, for very good reasons, rejected this view. But since, according to the Anglo-Catholics, they continued to identify the sacrifice of Christ with his death, the result was a negative attitude toward the idea of sacrifice in the Lord's Supper. The Reformation became negatively dependent on the theory it rejected.

In contrast to this identification of sacrifice and death the Anglican theologians propose a wider view of the sacrifice of Christ. This view embraces the whole earthly life of the Lord from his incarnation to his death. But this sacrifice which began when "the Logos became flesh" was not finished at his death. It continues in his heavenly existence as he, the great High Priest, continually offers his sacrifice on the heavenly altar. But because the sacrifice continues in heaven, it continues also on earth at the altars where the sacrament is celebrated. This line of argument implies that the activity in the sacrifice connected with the Lord's Supper is the activity of Christ. But at this point a transposition takes place. Now the idea is presented that we, the church, offer Christ, or his sacrifice. This transposition becomes possible because the church is vaguely identified with Christ. We observed above that Ramsey thus justifies the idea that we offer Christ. The same reasoning is found in Dix. He holds that because of the unity of the church with Christ, the eucharist of the church may be spoken of as a sacrifice of Christ. Thus the argument reaches its final point: the act of the church is Christ's own act; the church's offering is Christ's own offering, an offering of Christ or of his sacrifice.

When we define our attitude to these lines of thought, we must first of all emphasize that the Anglican or Anglo-Catholic contributions to ecumenical conversation about the Lord's Supper, which we have reviewed above, have greatly enriched the theological deliberations of the ecumenical movement. These documents have really presented points of view which are worthy of notice, and which may lead to fruitful discussions. Nor can we deny that in these contributions, at least in part, we meet ideas which are strictly biblical, but which have been obscured in both the Lutheran and the Reformed communions. In the critical analysis of their interpretation of the eucharist which I now present it is not my intention to engage in apologetics. How these Anglican theologians judge the Reformation has already been presented in the second section of this book. My purpose is to find, on the basis of the Bible, what the sacrifice means as a central element in the celebration of the Lord's Supper. In this way I hope to contribute something to a fruitful discussion and to the effort of overcoming the so-called deadlock which the Anglican theologians so often mention.

We may start with the assertion that the interpretation of the eucharist has suffered because the sacrifice of Christ has been identified exclusively with his death. It is claimed that this exclusiveness has had opposite results. In Medieval theology it led to the theory of a repetition of the sacrifice on Golgotha; but in Reformation theology the result was a depreciation of the sacrifice in the Lord's Supper. This last assertion is surprising, since death and sacrifice—however we may regard the extent of the sacrifice of Christ—cannot very well be placed in opposition to one another. A strong emphasis on his death must mean a strong emphasis on his sacrifice. An obvious result of the exclusive emphasis on his death, however, would be the elimination, or at least the weakening, of the conception of the living and exalted Lord. That such an antithesis cannot be found in Luther is clearly evident from our discussion of the Reformation in Part II.

The Anglican theologians do not mean, however, that the idea

of the sacrifice of Christ has been removed from the interpretation
of the Lord's Supper in the Reformation. They mean rather that
the sacrifice of Christ has become a historical event, something that
belongs in the past. As such it is a presupposition of the Lord's
Supper, but it has no immediate and present connection with the
sacrament. This would mean that the remembrance, anamnesis, in
question is conceived of as a recalling to memory of this past act of
sacrifice. We do not deny that an exclusive emphasis on the
sacrificial death may, and often has, caused "the remembrance"
to become a mere exercise of memory without the immediate
relationship to the sacrifice of Christ implied in the biblical conception of anamnesis. If, however, our interpretation of Luther's conception of the real presence is correct, this error cannot be attributed
to him. His insistence on the real presence of the body and blood
of Christ under bread and wine implies rather an accentuation of
the sacrifice of Christ. It is nevertheless understandable why the
Anglican theologians have characterized Luther's and the other
Reformers' attitude to the idea of sacrifice in the Lord's Supper
as "negative." Even if the sacrifice of Christ is present in the Lord's
Supper because Christ himself is present, this point has not been
directly and clearly expressed. The sacrifice of Christ is present,
so to speak, under the guise of "the real presence." Luther does
not speak directly about it. In reality he has a positive attitude, but
formally it appears as negative. His reluctance is due to his intense
struggle with contemporary corruptions of the gospel. The claim
that the church's celebration of the sacrament involved a repetition
of Christ's sacrifice on Golgotha had made the idea itself and the
terminology suspect. Consequently Luther does not speak directly
about the presence of the sacrifice of Christ in the Lord's Supper,
but the idea is there nevertheless in a different form.

As we have seen, the Anglican theologians assert that the restriction of sacrifice to the death on the cross leads to a one-sided conception and to a deadlock in the discussion from which we must

try to escape. Instead of this conception of the sacrifice as a point in time they insist that it is necessary to conceive of it in a larger perspective. His act of sacrifice includes his whole life here on earth from the incarnation; and his resurrection and exaltation signify the commencement of his continual sacrifice as the heavenly High Priest. Because of this continued sacrifice there is also a continuous sacrifice in the Lord's Supper. These assertions contain a number of problems which we must now discuss.

That Christ's act of sacrifice includes his whole life from the incarnation to his death is a valid and important point of view. It is clearly biblical. To restrict his sacrifice to his death on the cross would in reality obscure the significance of the sacrificial act of Christ. It would obscure its quality and character as a self-sacrifice in obedience to the will of the heavenly Father and in unbroken solidarity with humanity. Death becomes significant only if it is seen as the last and final act in connection with this continuous act of sacrifice. It is extremely important that the incarnation be conceived of as the starting point of the sacrificial act of Christ. Only then does it become clear that Christ's work of reconciliation is God's own work. God does not only "sacrifice" by sending his Son into the world, but also, to use Paul's words, "God was in Christ reconciling the world to himself." The expiation, the satisfaction of Christ, is a part of this context. It means not only that Christ in his human solidarity and on behalf of humanity vicariously endured God's judgment and the punishment due to sin, but primarily that he has fulfilled God's redemptive love. Concentration on his death, on the contrary, stands in the context of a different view of the atonement which regards his death as a quasi-juridical compensation presented to God: a doctrine of the atonement typical of Medieval thinking, which has exercised a continuous influence even in Reformation theology.

It is, however, not at all true that an emphasis on the death on the cross is the same as an isolation of the death-sacrifice. The

New Testament is decisive on this point. No one will deny that both the Gospels and the Epistles emphasize the death on the cross to the greatest possible degree, but this emphasis in no sense isolates his death from the rest of the work of Christ. What the New Testament primarily wants to say is that the sacrifice of Christ was finished in his death. In this act he finished the work for which he had come into the world. The victory was manifested in the resurrection and the exaltation. The exaltation is God's "yes" to the perfect sacrifice which now once for all was consummated, completed, and finished. It need not be repeated, and it cannot be complemented in any way. Through this one atoning sacrifice all other atonements, or attempts at atonement, have been eliminated. This one sacrifice has made satisfaction for all time and for all generations, because it was at the same time the sacrifice of Christ and God's own sacrifice. When the New Testament uses the word sacrifice in other connections, when it speaks of the sacrifice of praise and prayer, or when Paul says that we are to "present our bodies a living sacrifice, holy and acceptable to God," the word has an entirely different connotation and significance from that sacrifice which Christ made once for all.

This view of the sacrifice of Christ as definitive is fundamental for the New Testament. This is the central point of the kerygma. This sacrifice has caused a radical change in God's relationship to the world. The new covenant has been established. The new age of reconciliation has dawned. This radical change has affected Christ himself. He is no longer God's Suffering Servant, he is the victorious Lord. The ascension was his coronation. He has "entered into his glory" (Luke 24:26) as the King in *Regnum Christi*. Thus the New Testament ties together the death on the cross and the exaltation. The proclamation is really a *theologia crucis*, but at the same time a *theologia gloriae Christi*.

When the New Testament depicts for us the heavenly Christ, it presents him not only as the King sitting on the right hand of

God but also as the High Priest. The Letter to the Hebrews unites these two aspects (Heb. 8:1). We are indebted to the Anglican theologians for their strong accentuation of the high priestly perspective, which has not always been given due recognition. It is also proper that they have emphasized the connection between the eternal priesthood of Christ in heaven and the celebration of the eucharist on earth. However, there may be some risks connected with this interpretation of his office as High Priest in heaven. The conception of Christ as the One who continually serves at the heavenly altar tends to suggest that the heavenly "offering" is of the same type as his sacrifice here on earth "in the days of his flesh," that it is a continuation of this sacrifice, and that it has the same significance. Even if this is by no means the intention of these theologians, the terms that they use tend in that direction. But in that case the reality of the radical change mentioned above would be obscured. Just as it is essential to recognize that, according to the biblical view, Christ is ever active in completing his work of redemption, so it is equally essential to maintain that his redemptive sacrifice is definitive, and that we cannot speak of its continuation. Through the exaltation God has spoken his "yes" to the sacrifice made once for all. He does not continue to offer his Son, and the Son does not continue as the Suffering Servant of the Lord to give himself as he did during his earthly life.

The biblical document which speaks most fully of Christ's activity as High Priest connects it both with the sacrifice made once for all and with the prayer of intercession for his own. When the Letter to the Hebrews insists again and again that the sacrifice made once for all is final and valid, it does not thereby relegate it to the past. On the contrary, the past is here also the present. The emphasis on the fact that the sacrifice has been finished once for all signifies that it is eternally valid and therefore eternally present. Christ's act of sacrifice is one with himself. His sacrifice is and remains a living and effective reality in his person. Therefore, since the ascended Lord is not limited by time and space, his sacrifice is effectively present in the Lord's Supper, where the Lord under bread and wine has designated a meeting place with the people of the new covenant, his church on earth.

The intercession of the heavenly High Priest, recorded not only in Hebrews but also in John, testifies to our Lord's solidarity with his body, the church. This intercession is a part of the Lord's continued activity whereby he actualizes the work of redemption in and through his church; or, in other words, it is a part of his continued activity to create and give life. It is not a continuation of his sacrifice which was perfected and finished in his death, but rests on the foundation of that sacrifice, because its presupposition is the new covenant which was established when God was in Christ reconciling the world to himself. The intercession of the heavenly High Priest is related to the total life of the church, and not least to Holy Communion, which from one point of view is the church's essential act of prayer. We enclose our prayers in the intercessory prayer of Christ. He receives them and unites them with his mighty intercession.

After this discussion of the heavenly High Priest we return to the question of sacrifice in the Lord's Supper. If the sacrifice offered once for all is eternally valid and relevant, and if it is one with Christ who is himself the sacrifice, then the presence of Christ in the sacrament includes the effective presence of his sacrifice. It is not a question of recalling something which happened two thousand years ago on Golgotha. The past is here, too, the present, as the Lord himself makes the past and eternally valid sacrifice contemporaneous with us. As the Lord on that last evening of his life presented the sacrifice which was momentarily to be made, and which signified the last act in his total sacrificial activity, and as he included his disciples in his sacrifice and united them with it, so also he includes his present disciples in the sacrifice which is eternally valid and eternally effective, and makes them partakers of the blessings flowing from the sacrament. It is significant that the effective presence of the sacrifice of Christ in the eucharist has been emphasized in the ecumenical discussions, not least by the Anglicans. In view of this fact we must insist that the presence of the sacrifice is inseparately connected with the presence of the living Lord. The real presence and the sacrifice belong together. *This sacrifice is present because the living Lord is present. But the living Lord cannot be present without actualizing his sacrifice.* Because he is the *living* Lord who unites us with his sacrifice, he also makes us partakers of his victory. He receives us into the new age and blesses us "with every spiritual blessing in the heavenly places" (Eph. 1:3). The participation in Christ given us in the Lord's Supper means that we die with Christ and rise with him, dying to the old age and participating in the life of the new age through the power of the resurrection of Christ.

But the Anglo-Catholic theologians do not want to speak only of the presence of the sacrifice in the sacrament; they want to connect this sacrifice of Christ with our action by formulas such as: with the eucharistic elements we "offer Christ" or "offer his sacrifice," so that we thus participate in that sacrifice which he himself offers at the heavenly altar. We have already discussed this idea, but it is necessary to ask a few additional questions. What religious significance can be found in such formulas? Why are they so insistent on using them?

Men like Ramsey and Hebert are fully conscious of the fact that such formulas may easily suggest associations which are both dangerous and destructive. These formulas have been associated with suggestions that our offering of Christ is a meritorious act, that his sacrifice needs to be complemented by continuous sacrifices, that God is really not reconciled, and that he must be propitiated by our continually offering Christ. We need hardly say that such ideas which destroy the gospel are not held by the Anglo-Catholic theologians. They agree fully with the Reformers that the founda-

tion of our salvation is the grace of God alone and not any merit
of our own. As we have seen, Hebert insists that the statement
that we offer Christ in the sacrament is completely compatible
with the Reformation doctrine of justification by faith alone, and
he rejects all associations which point in another direction. Those
who defend the formula of our offering Christ may, of course, tell
us that a theological statement ought not to be rejected simply
because erroneous associations have become attached to it. The
Reformation doctrine of justification by faith has led to many
erroneous interpretations, among others that faith has been regarded
as somehow a meritorious work. Such a defense may be accepted
provided the statement concerned contains unquestionable religious value. In that case we must adhere to it, even if its preserva-
tion necessitates that many misinterpretations be rejected. The
question is then whether the statement that "the church offers
Christ, or his sacrifice, in the sacrament" has any such unmistakable
religious significance.

What may be the significance of the statement that "we offer
Christ in the eucharist"? We are reminded that this question was
asked in the preface to the English edition of the book by the Roman theologian Masure, *Le Sacrifice du Chef* (see above, p. 49ff).
The preface states that people seldom hear sermons on the mass
which really explain why the sacrifice is offered and what it is
all about. In a certain sense this may be a testimony that it is not
so very easy to give a clear answer to this question. The translator
maintains, however, that Masure has actually supplied the answer.
It is interesting to compare his answer to that given by Hebert to
the same question. The significance of our offering consists, according to Masure, partly in that our adoration through the offering
of "Christ and the cross" becomes perfected, and partly in that
we in this offering, because of the divine act of transubstantiation,
receive a sure proof of the sufficiency of the divine redemption.
In reference to the first statement we ask whether the idea that

our thanksgiving and adoration become "perfect" does not anticipate the perfection of the new age. The second statement points
to the transubstantiation as a transformation of the offering of the
church into the sacrifice of Christ himself. In this way, as we have
already pointed out, the accent is moved from the offering of the
church to the change performed by God. Strictly speaking, therefore, it is not the church which offers Christ, but God who transforms the offering of the church so that it becomes Christ's own
sacrifice, or Christ himself.

We have already observed Hebert's interpretation of what it
means that in the eucharist we present the sacrifice of Christ (see
above, p. 28ff). We will not repeat here the discussion of his
views, but we must add a few remarks. We have established that
it is not a question in any real sense of our offering Christ or his
sacrifice. Hebert presented his thesis by saying that in the sacrament we present our weak and insufficient intercessory prayers. In
so doing we hold up before God Christ's own sacrifice, his death
for our salvation, the love of Christ as it exists objectively in his
intercession and in the sacrament which he has given to us. We
include our intercession in his intercession and in his sacrifice. In
reality this is just an interpretation of what it means to pray in
the name of Jesus. It is not really a question of our offering Christ.
We rely on his sacrificial love, we become incorporated into his
sacrifice and participate in it, but we do not offer Christ. The only
expression used by Hebert which might suggest this meaning is
the statement, "in the sacrament I hold up before God Christ's
own sacrifice."

The significance of such a formula is certainly not that God
is an unreconciled God whom we propitiate by bringing before
him the sacrifice of Christ as our own sacrifice. The intention is
not to separate God and Christ in such a way that judgment and
wrath belong to God and love belongs to Christ, as if God were
not love, and Christ were not to judge sin. The meaning is rather

that we rely on the sacrifice of Christ which he now presents and makes relevant to us in the sacrament. We hold to this sacrifice because it is a sacrifice of love, and because this love is God's own love. This line of thought is the same as that which confronts us in I John: "By this we know love, that he laid down his life for us." We take refuge in the sacrifice of Christ because there we have learned to know what we did not otherwise know: the love of God which here is revealed in action as an actual, living reality. But when we introduce the formula of offering Christ or his sacrifice in the sacrament, we do not express this religious content. It is not a question of our offering Christ. The use of this formula indicates a shift in ideas, which is made easier by the employment of such terms as "present," "plead," "hold up," etc., in a sense more or less synonymous with "sacrifice."

If there is, therefore, a contradiction between this formula that we offer Christ in the sacrament and the interpretation which is given to it, we must ask why some are so anxious to use this formula. The answer is that this depends on the power of "tradition." This manner of speaking about the presence of the sacrifice of Christ in the sacrament is supposed to belong to "the catholic tradition."

We must then ask ourselves what is understood by the terms "catholic" and "catholicity." An investigation indicates that they can be used in two different senses. They can be interpreted historically and be connected with certain definite communions; but they can also be interpreted in principle, or according to their essential meaning. The former of these interpretations is of ancient usage. The church was called catholic even during the primitive period. As long as the church was undivided, the term did not indicate a contrast, except in the case of small, heretical movements. But this situation changed at the time of the great separation in the Reformation. The churches of the Reformation were characterized as "Protestant" in contrast to "Catholic" Rome. The terms "Catholic" and "Protestant" were thus applied to different sections of the divided church. The reason why these Anglican theologians now seek to preserve the "catholic" tradition of sacrifice is associated with their desire to maintain that the Anglican communion belongs among the "catholic" churches. By this they do not deny that it is a reformed church. They are interested in a conception of the church as both reformed and catholic, a conception which enables them to maintain contacts in several directions. They do not speak of reformed and catholic in order to separate the two, but to unite them. Nevertheless this division of the various communions into two principal categories is a sign of separation. Such a division establishes boundaries. It is not strange, therefore, that this division has caused considerable difficulties in ecumenical discussions.

But we may consider the terms catholic and catholicity also from the point of view of their essential meaning. These Anglican theologians also use them in this sense. Thus Ramsey says that the word catholic "is often linked to piety which is individualistic, and to systems which are sectarian and incomplete."[1] "Catholicity" thus is no longer a standard whereby boundaries may be drawn between various communions. There is no guarantee that because a communion designates itself "catholic," it has retained "true" catholicity. Ramsey notes that the Roman Counter-Reformation did not retain "the real meaning of the word catholic," and "some of the uncatholic tendencies of the Middle Ages were continued and even deepened in the revival which was led and organized by the Council of Trent." They did not rediscover "the organic view of the church and its worship," the church as the body of Christ. This is amply supported by Rome's institutionalism and individualism. In the Vatican Council, 1870, institutionalism triumphed over the organic view of the church. The individualism in the piety of the Counter-Reformation appears not least in the celebration of the

[1] *Ibid.*, p. 174.

eucharist, where the liturgy is regarded as the offering of a sacrifice, in which the participation of the congregation consists mostly in private devotion; communion becomes a private act separated from the liturgy; and adoration may be equally private and focused upon the presence of the Lord in the Blessed Sacrament reserved in the tabernacle.[2] We may note parenthetically that modern efforts toward liturgical reformation within the Roman church seek to overcome the tendencies which are the object of Ramsey's criticism.

It is evident that in the sense in which we have now discussed the term, catholicity is no longer a quantitative but a qualitative idea. There is a "true" catholicity, but there are also misinterpretations of it. A departure from the "true" catholicity involves therefore a departure from that which is "genuine" and "essential" Christianity, from that which characterizes the nature of the Christian message, and from that which ought to characterize the life in the church which is the body of Christ. In this meaning catholicity ceases to be a term which divides Christendom. Instead it creates fellowship. In other words, it becomes ecumenical.

After this analysis of the idea of catholicity we return to the question whether the eucharist can be designated as our offering of Christ or of his sacrifice. Can we truly say that this formula expresses a "true" catholicity? It is difficult to understand how it would be possible to maintain such a view. To be sure, such a formula appears relatively early, in the writings of Cyprian in the third century, although its meaning was not then definitely fixed. But from that time on an appeal can be made to a long tradition. But this does not prove its true catholicity. The formula does not occur in either the New Testament or in the documents of the primitive church. This fact naturally does not prevent it from being catholic. It would be acceptable anyway, provided it were in line with and could be regarded as an interpretation of the New Testament. But in reality it is contrary to the fundamental con-

[2] *Ibid.*, p. 171ff.

ception of the sacrifice of Christ which we find in the New Testament. The sacrifice of Christ is entirely and solely his sacrifice— and God's. This is the one essential point: God was in Christ reconciling the world to himself. Through this sacrifice perfected once for all he abolished all man-made sacrifices. A formula such as this that we "offer Christ" turns the biblical kerygma upside down. It is not strange, therefore, that all kinds of erroneous associations have become attached to it. Nor is it strange that the Anglican theologians who have adopted it can use it only by giving it a meaning differing from the literal, and by reinterpreting it in the light of their insight into the real significance of the gospel.

After we have said this, however, it is exceedingly important to emphasize the fundamental significance of the idea of sacrifice in the sacrament and in the celebration of the Lord's Supper in the church. Such an emphasis is in accordance with true catholicity. But then it must be evident that we are concerned first of all with the sacrifice of Christ.

It is true, however, that we both can and ought to speak of our "offering" in the sacrament. The Lord's Supper is not only an act of Christ, it is also an action which we, the church of Christ on earth, perform in obedience to his word: "do this." But what we in this connection call an offering lies on a different plane and has another significance than the sacrifice of Christ. His sacrifice is the foundation, the prerequisite, and the cause of everything that we may call our "sacrifice," whether it be thanksgiving and praise, prayer and intercession, or willing service. The Lord's Supper is the church's eucharist, its great service of thanksgiving, in which the church of Christ on earth unites its humble offering of praise with the great paean of praise in heaven. The Lord's Supper is the church's incomparable act of prayer in which we include our prayers in the intercession of our great High Priest. Holy Communion does not at all mean that the disciples of the Lord are removed from the world. The Lord who here deals with his own does not isolate them from the world of God's creation. He sends them out to serve his purposes. The love of Christ constrains us.

But no matter how important and essential this our part may be, the sacrifice in the eucharist is pre-eminently the sacrifice of Christ. This connection was there when the Lord supped with his disciples on the last evening of his life. The connection with this sacrifice gave and gives the central content to the eucharist, because, through God's affirmation in the resurrection and the exaltation, the sacrifice of Christ becomes eternally valid. When the living Lord meets his own in Holy Communion, he actualizes the sacrifice anew in the gifts of bread and wine. As the Lord on the last evening included and incorporated his disciples in his sacrifice of love about to be perfected in death, so now he includes his disciples everywhere and in all times in the eternally valid sacrifice and in the new covenant established in his death. This participation involves dying to the old age and walking in the newness of life. In this sense it involves "dying with Christ" and "living in the power of his resurrection" (Phil. 3:10). The sacrifice of Christ is victory. The Lord who is present in the Lord's Supper and there deals with his church is the heavenly Victor.

18

Mysterium Christi

In our study we have noted a number of different perspectives of the Lord's Supper, or various kinds of eucharistic motifs. These reflect in various ways the tremendous riches found in the sacrament of the altar. We may compare what we see to a display of variegated colors. Here are the gray of suffering, the red of shed blood, the blue of faith and fellowship with Christ, the green of hope, and the white of the heavenly Lord and of the eucharist. But all these "motifs" constitute together an inseparable unity. From whatever perspective we look at the Lord's Supper, it is one mighty act which presents the gospel of God clearly and visibly before our eyes.

The conflicts between the various interpretations of the Lord's Supper which have appeared in the history of the church have to a great extent been caused by the isolation of one or another aspect of the sacrament. Because one aspect has been removed from its context, it has come in conflict with other aspects and has become false and one-sided. We have found one example of this within the New Testament itself in the docetic-spiritualistic interpretation and the caricature of the eucharistic element which Paul attacked in Corinth. We must therefore say something of the essential unity of these aspects which in the course of time have appeared in a certain tension or even conflict with one another.

We turn first to the question of the relationship between *sacrifice and communion*. The later Middle Ages regarded the Lord's Supper primarily as the church's act of sacrifice. In this way it obscured the communion aspect. But this aspect received new life in the Reformation. The objection to the Reformation, however, has been that it neglected the idea of sacrifice. Formally this objection is no doubt correct. But in our discussion of the Reformation in Part II we have indicated what the situation really was in this respect, and we need not repeat it here. Yet it is important to notice the essential connection between sacrifice and communion. The communion which is realized in Holy Communion is inseparably connected with the sacrifice of Christ. This significance of the Lord's Supper as communion becomes imperiled when Christ's own sacrifice in reality is set aside in favor of an emphasis on an offering of Christ which the church is supposed to make. By so doing we obscure both the fact that the new covenant is a living reality through the sacrifice made once for all, and the fact that Christ unites the guests in a communion with himself by actualizing his eternally valid sacrifice and making it present in the sacrament. This fellowship with Christ is at the same time also communion in and with his church, a fellowship which embraces both the church militant on earth and "the heavenly Jerusalem, . . . the assembly of the first-born who are enrolled in heaven" (Heb. 12:22-23).

Sacrifice and eucharist. "The first conflict about the Lord's Supper" came because the eucharistic element was emphasized at the expense of the sacrifice, and thus it became a caricature. The essential unity of sacrifice and eucharist is evident already in the fact that our eucharistic thanksgiving and praise are directed to "the Lamb that was slain," the living Lord who because of his perfect and eternally valid sacrifice is worthy to receive "blessing and honor and glory." But in reality the Lord's last meal with his disciples combines eucharist and sacrifice. Christ himself made this sacrificial meal a eucharist when "he took a cup, and when he had given thanks he gave it to them" (Mark 14:23). The holy act is surrounded with thanksgiving and is itself an act of thanksgiving, a eucharist. In this connection we may properly quote the words of Jesus as he contemplates the sacrifice on the cross: "The hour has come for the Son of man to be glorified" (John 12:23).

Sacrifice and the real presence. The Lord's Supper combines the sacrifice and the real presence in an inseparable unity. They cannot be separated, but neither can they be identified. The Christ who is present in the Lord's Supper is the living Lord. Since he exists as the heavenly, living Lord, he cannot be present in any other way. The possibility of his presence depends on the fact that he is the ascended Lord who sits on the right hand of the Father, and that he is therefore independent of the limitations of time and space. But this does not mean that his presence is separated from his sacrifice. On the contrary, the living Lord who is present in the eucharist is none other than the Crucified. The finished and eternally valid sacrifice cannot be separated from him. When he comes in the Holy Communion, he actualizes the sacrifice of the new covenant and makes it effectively present. That he has connected his presence with the bread and the wine signifies that the sacrifice of his body and blood becomes effectively present, and that he comes "with every spiritual blessing in the heavenly places."

When sacrifice and presence are separated, the presence of the Lord becomes conceived of in a spiritual sense. It does not become concrete in the Lord's Supper, and therefore is not a real presence in the essential meaning of this word. The bread and the wine are then regarded as symbols of the sacrifice which was fulfilled in his death, but as symbols only in the sense of a reminder, not as effective signs or symbols which contain the reality and realize that of which they are symbols. Anamnesis in that case becomes limited to our attempt to recall something that once happened in the past.

If now, on the other hand, the sacrifice and the real presence are identified, the result is an apparently strong emphasis on the presence of Christ, since in that case the bread and the wine are "changed" into and identified with the sacrifice of Christ's body and blood. But in reality the real presence ceases then to be the presence of the living Lord, and is reduced to an impersonal presence. As a consequence the way is opened for the conception that the sacrifice is something which we, the church, control and administer.

We do not need to choose between separating or identifying the sacrifice and the real presence. Such an alternative indicates a wrong approach. This is not the only time that conflicts and difficulties in regard to the interpretation of the Lord's Supper have arisen because of a wrong approach. The same thing happens when the alternative of individualism or collectivism is applied to the Lord's Supper. It may be true, as Ramsey emphasizes, that communion piety in the later Middle Ages was overwhelmingly individualistic. The same has often been true of the Protestant communions during the periods of both Orthodoxy and Pietism. Wherever such an exclusive individualism appears, it indicates a lack of perception of the church as the body of Christ. The background of Medieval individualism was the substitution of a rigid institutionalism for the living, biblical view of the church as the body of Christ. The situation was to some extent similar within Protestant Orthodoxy. Pietistic individualism was connected with a truncated view of the church as belonging primarily to individual believers. When the church is understood as the body of Christ, the vine with living branches, the temple of living stones, there is no room for either extreme individualism or exclusive institutionalism. It then becomes self-evident that the action in the Lord's Supper involves every individual Christian, as the act of communion indicates. But it also becomes self-evident that Christ in the eucharist deals with his church as a whole, and that this Holy Communion is the joint action of the church. Where the Lord's Supper is celebrated, there we find the church of Christ in action.

Another wrong and inadequate approach is the attempt to *differentiate between the means of grace*. We have touched on this subject before (p. 67ff). One of the great achievements of the

Reformation was the rediscovery of the Word as a means of grace. But the reformer who made this rediscovery never asked the question which means of grace should be regarded as the greatest: the Word or the sacraments. Essentially there could be for him no depreciation of either baptism or the Lord's Supper; both are the Lord's action with his church and in his church. Later on the question of preference was often raised within Protestant communions. There is no more wisdom in this question than in the question of the disciples as to who is the greatest in the kingdom of God. In many places the result was that the Lord's Supper was assigned an obscure place in the worship life of the church. The question is unreasonable because the Lord's Supper includes in itself the mighty Word of Christ. The Holy Communion makes the whole wealth of the gospel living and concrete in all its fulness.

We have seen that conflicts and difficulties in the interpretation of the Lord's Supper are closely connected with a wrong approach to the subject. These approaches are very often connected with a conscious or unconscious attempt to rationalize the mystery of the sacrament. This happens because the presence of Christ is either materialized or spiritualized. In the former the Christ present in the sacrament is identified with the elements. This identification represents a desire to make the Christ present in the Lord's Supper an object of sight, so that we anticipate the situation in the world to come, when faith is replaced by sight. In a contrary sense, a spiritualizing conception results in a separation of the heavenly Christ from the action in the sacrament. The Lord's Supper becomes then a symbolic act. But the symbol does not include the reality. The significance becomes a recollection of what once happened and a suggestion of what is going to happen again in the future.

It is of course true that these two perspectives are closely related. The Lord's Supper calls attention to that which has happened once for all, to the sacrifice perfected in death which established the new covenant and constitutes the basis for every celebration of the Lord's Supper in the church. But it also directs attention to that which is to come, to the fulfilment in the Parousia of Christ, and to "the great supper in heaven." The eschatological perspective is inseparably connected with the eucharist. It is an eschatological feast, as it is expressed in the ancient Christian prayer: *Maranatha,* our Lord, come!

But the eschatological perspective is not limited to that which is to come. What is above all characteristic is that the two perspectives, that which has happened and that which is going to happen, are tied together in what may be called the eschatological present. The great heavenly High Priest, who is a high priest for ever "according to the order of Melchizedek," makes his once-for-all and eternally valid sacrifice effectively present when in the Lord's Supper he give us the bread of life and the cup of blessing. He permits us here and now to taste "the powers of the age to come" (Heb. 6:5). The new age of life, which is going to be fulfilled, has come in him, and its "powers" are active where he is at work. What we have now in faith, in this world of sin and death, is an earnest of that which will be given "in the life of the world to come."

But the reason why that which has happened and that which will happen can be tied together with that which now happens in the Lord's Supper is that the living Lord himself is present and active in his church. The thing of paramount importance, as it has often been stated in the documents from the various churches, is that the Lord himself is the true celebrant in the eucharist. It is regrettable that we do not always take this statement seriously and put it into practice. This statement is obscured as soon as the idea arises that the sacrifice of Christ is something that we can control instead of something in which we trust. But it is also obscured when we regard "heavenly worship" as in some sense parallel with the celebration of the eucharist here on earth. In so doing we emphasize the distance between "the heavenly" and "the earthly" in a way which ignores the fact that the heavenly High Priest himself officiates at the earthly altar, and thereby ties together the heavenly and the earthly in a great, unfathomable mystery.

At this point, the mystery of Christ in the Lord's Supper, we have to stop. One of the letters in the New Testament introduces the confession of Christ with these words: "Great indeed, we confess, is the mystery of our religion" (I Tim. 3:16). The first and the last lines in this confession speak of Christ as "manifested in the flesh" and "taken up in glory." In the same way the Christ-mystery of the eucharist is enclosed between the incarnation and the glorification. The seal of this mystery is broken. Its revealed secret is nothing else than the mystery of God's gracious love which has been revealed in Christ. But the mystery does not disappear when it has been revealed. On the contrary, the more it is revealed to us, the more fully we behold the mystery in its unspeakable depth.

Index

Index

Type used in this book
Body, 11 on 13 Garamond
Display, Garamond

Paper: Old Style Wove